Muslims' Afflictions

[a study of causes and their remedy]

by

Maulana MUHAMMAD ZAKARIYYA Shaikhul Hadith

Translated by : **Iftikhar Ahmed 'Alavi**

Revised & Edited by : **Sadruddin 'Amir Ansari**

KITAB BHAVAN

New Delhi-110002

KITAB BHAVAN
Publishers, Exporters & Importers
1784, Kalan Mahal, Darya Ganj
New Delhi - 110 002 [India]

Phones : 3274686, 3263383
Telex : 31-63106 ALI IN
Fax : 91-11-3263383

ISBN 81-7151-198-8

Reprinted 1994

Published by:
Nusrat Ali Nasri for Kitab Bhavan
1784, Kalan Mahal, Darya Ganj
New Delhi - 110 002 [India]

Printed in India at:
F.M. Offset Printers
Kalan Mahal, Darya Ganj
New Delhi - 110 002 [India]

بسم الله الرحمن الرحيم

CONTENTS

SCHEME OF TRANSLITERATION

Short Vowels

(Fatḥah)	(ـَ)	a
(Kasirah)	(ـِ)	i
(Dammah)	(ـُ)	u

ا	Consonantal sound	a	A
ا	Long Vowel	ā	Ā
ب		b	B
ت		t	T
ث		th	TH
ج		j	J
ح		ḥ	Ḥ
خ		kh	KH
د		d	D
ذ		dh	DH
ر		r	R
ز		z	Z
س		s	S
ش		sh	SH
ص		ṣ	Ṣ
ض		ḍ	Ḍ
ط		ṭ	T
ظ		z	Z
ع		‘	‘
غ		gh	GH
ف		f	F
ق		q	Q
ک		k	K
ل		l	L
م		m	M
ن		n	N
ھ ہ		h	H
و	consonant	w	W
و	long vowel	ū	U
و	dipthong	au	AU
ی	consonant	y	Y
ی	long vowel	ī	I
ے	dipthong	ai	AI

بسم الله الرحمن الرحيم

EDITOR'S FOREWORD

نَحْمَدُهٗ وَنُصَلِّيْ وَنُسَلِّمُ عَلٰى رَسُوْلِهِ الْكَرِيْمِ

I am highly thankful to Allah the Almighty to present this book to reader. It is a fulfilment of my longfelt desire. I think Mr. Iftikhar Ahmed can justifiably compliment himself on rendering this extremely useful and valuable material into English. The preface by the translator fully explains the value of the book and I must not say anything more, nor the author of the original Urdụ text Ḥadrat Shaikhul Ḥadīth Maulana Muhammad Zakariyya Ṣahib needs any introduction by such an ordinary man like me. He is well-known everywhere. I would, however, take the opportunity to give here a list of his important works. May he live long among us !

May the Almighty accept this service and grant His Blessings on the author, the translator, the editor, the publisher and all those who co-operated in some way or the other in presenting this English version to readers.

SADRUDDĪN 'ĀMIR ANṢĀRĪ

LIST OF WORKS OF HADRAT SHAIKHUL ḤADĪTH MAULANA MUHAMMAD ZAKARIYYA

ARABIC WORKS (Published)

S. No.

1. (I) AUJAZ UL-MASĀLIK SHARH-I-MU'ATTĀ AL-IMĀM-I-MĀLIK

6 Vols. Price : Rs. 100/- Tradition. Period of compilation :—1/3/1345 A.H.—28/12/1375 A.H. (31 Years) (Letho printing)

2. (II) JUZ'U ḤAJJAT-IL-WADĀ' WA 'UMARĀT-UL-NABĪ, Ṣallallāhu 'Alaihi Wa Sallam. Tradition. Period of compilation :—Part 1 : 22nd Rabī-'ul Awwal, 1341 A.H.—23rd Rabī-'ul Awwal, 1341 A.H. Part II : Thursday, 17th Jamādil-Ulā, 1390 A.H.—Friday, 15th Rajab, 1390 A.H. Letho printing and then in modern Arabic type printing, price : Rs. 15/-

3. (III) ALKAUKAB-UL-DURRĪ 2 parts, price : Rs. 20/- Tradition, period of compilation :—Part I completed by the middle of Rabī'ul Awwal, 1352 A.H. Part II completed by 16/7/1353 A.H. (Letho)

4. (IV) LĀMI UD DARĀRĪ 3 Vols. Price : Rs. 60/- Tradition. Period of compilation :—7/1/1376 A.H.—10/3/1388 A.H. (Letho)

5. (V) MUQADDIMAH AUJAZ-UL-MASĀLIK Tradition. Introduction to No. I published separately in modern Arabic type, price : Rs. 12/-

6. (VI) MUQADIMAH LĀMI 'UDDARĀRĪ, Tradition, Introduction to No. 4 published separately in modern Arabic type. Price : Rs. 20/-

7. (VII) AL-ABWĀB-U-WAT-TARĀJIM LIL-BUKHĀRĪ Tradition. (Letho, and then in type) Price : Rs. 6/-

ARABIC WORKS (UNPUBLISHED)

8. (I) TALKHĪṢ-ul-BADHL (Summary of the Badhlul Majhūd, the famous commentary of late Maulānā Khalīl Aḥmed on Sunani-Abī Dā'ūd). Tradition. Period of compilation :—Rabī'ul Awwal 1335 A.H.—1345 A.H., during the compilation of Badhlul Majhūd.

9. (II) SHADHARĀT-ul-ḤADĪTH Tradition. Period of compilation :—1335 A.H.—1345 A.H. during the compilation of Badhlul Majhūd.

10. (III) HAWĀSHĪ BADHLUL-MAJHŪD Tradition
Period of compilation :—1340 A.H.—1388 A.H.
(Explanatory notes on Badhlul Majhūd)

11. (IV) MUQUDDIMĀT-i-KUTUB-i-HADĪTH Tradition
(Introductions to various works of traditions)

12. (V) MU'JAMUL-MUSNAD-LIL--IMĀM AHMAD
Alphabetical Index of the Traditions.

13. (VI) JUZ'UL-MI'RĀJ (Incomplete), Tradition

14. (VII) JUZ'U WAFĀT-IN-NABI, Ṣallallāhu 'Alaihi Wa Sallam (incomplete), Tradition

15. (VIII) JUZ'U AFDALIL-A'MĀL (incomplete), Tradition

16. (IX) JUZ'U RIWĀYĀT-il-ISTIḤĀḌAH Tradition

17. (X) JUZ'U RAF'-il-YADAIN (incomplete) Tradition

18. (XI) JUZ'U AL-A'MĀLU BIN-NIYYĀT Tradition

19. (XII) JUZ'U IKHTILĀFĀT-IS-SALĀT Tradition

20. (XIII) JUZ'UL MUBHAMĀT FIL ASĀNĪD WAR-RIWĀYĀT, Tradition

21. (XIV) JUZ'U MUKAFFIRĀT-IDH-DHNŪB Tradition

22. (XV) JUZ'U MULTAQAṬ-il-MIRQĀT Tradition
Period of compilation :—Monday, 29/12/1341 A.H.—

23. (XVI) JUZ'U MULTAQAṬ—IR—RUWĀT 'AN-IL MIRQĀT Tradition. Period of compilation :— Last Friday of Dhi Qa'dah, 1341 A.H.—Monday 29th Dhul Ḥijjah, 1341 A.H.

24. (XVII) JUZ'UL MANĀṬ Tradition

25. (XVIII) JUZ'U ṢALĀT-il-ISTISQĀ' Tradition

26. (XIX) JUZ'U ṢALĀT-il-KHAUF Tradition

27. (XX) JUZ'U SALĀT-il-KUSŪF Tradition

28. (XXI) JUZ'U MĀ QĀLAL MUḤADDITHŪN FIL IMĀM il-A'ZAM Tradition

29. (XXII) JUZ'U TAKHRĪJ-I-'ĀISHAH (R.A) FĪ QIṢṢAT-I-BARĪRAH Tradition

30. (XXIII) JUZ'U 'UMARĀ'-I-MADĪNAH, Tradition

31. (XXIV) JUZ'U MĀ YUSHKALU 'ALAL-JĀRIḤĪN Tradition

32. (XXV) JUZ'U ṬURUQ—IL—MADĪNAH Tradition

33. (XXVI) JUZ'UL JIHĀD Tradition

34. (XXVII) JUZ'U ANKAHTU, Ṣallallāhu 'Alaihi Wasallam Tradition

35. (XXVIII) TAQRĪR-I-NASĀ'Ī SHARĪF Tradition, Period of compilation :—4/4/1341 A.H.—Friday, Jumāda Thānī 1341 A.H.

36. (XXIX) TAQRIR-i-MISHKĀTUL-MAṢĀBĪḤ Tradition Period of compilation:—Shawwāl, 1341 A.H.— (Lectures on Mishkāt)

37. (XXX) TAQĀRĪR-i-KUTUB-i-ḤADĪTH Tradition (Lectures on the books of traditions)

38. (XXXI) UṢUL-i-ḤADĪTH 'ALĀ MADHHABIL ḤANAFIYYAH Science of Traditions. Period of compilation:—8/5/1342 A H.—10/5/1342 A.H. (explanatory notes added till 1388 A.H.)

39. (XXXII) ḤAWĀSHĪ 'ALAL ISHĀ 'AH Tradition. Period of compilation :—1335 A H.——1388 A.H. (Explanatory notes on Al-Ishā'ah)

40. (XXXIII) ḤAWĀSHĪ DHAIL-UT-TAHDHĪB Biography of traditionists (Explanatory notes)

41. (XXXIV) ḤAWĀSHĪ MUSALSALĀT Tradition/Taṣawwuf Period of Compilation :—1353 A.H —1380 A H.

42. (XXXV) AULIYĀT-UL-QIYĀMAH Tradition

43. (XXXVI) MUKHATAṢṢĀT-UL-MISHKAT Tradition

44. (XXXVII) JĀMI '-UR-RIWĀYĀT WAL-AJZĀ' Tradition Period of compilation :— after 1335 A.H.—1388 A.H.

45. (XXXVIII) MU'JAM-U-RIJĀL-i-TADHKIRAT-il-ḤUFFĀZ —LIL DHAHABĪ Biography of Traditionists

46. (XXXIX) TABWIB-Ū-TĀWĪL MUKHATALAF-il-AḤĀDĪTH LIBN-I-QUTAIBAH Tradition. Date of compilation :— 5/5/1342 A.H. (Friday night)

47. (XL) TABWĪB-U-MUSHKIL-UL-ĀTHĀR Tradition

48. (XLI) MU'JAM-UṢ-ṢAḤĀBAT-IL-LATĪ AKHRAJA 'ANHUM ABŪ DĀ'ŪD-UT-TAYĀLISĪ FĪ MUSNADIHĪ Index of Traditions

49. (XLII) TABWĪB-U-AḤKĀM-il-QUR'ĀN LIL-JASSĀS Commentary on the Holy Qur'an.

50. (XLIII) SHARḤI 'ARABĪ JAZARĪ Recitation of the HOLY QUR'ĀN Period of compilation :—1345 A.H. (While the writer was sojourning in the city of the Prophet Ṣallallāhu 'Alaihi Wa Sallam)

51. (XLIV) RISĀLAH AḤWĀL-I-QURRĀ'I-SAB'AH Recitation of the HOLY QUR'AN.

52. (XLV) AL-BUDUR MA' NUJŪMIHIM-il-ARAB'ATA 'ASHAR Recitation of the HOLY QUR'AN.

53. (XLVI) IḌĀFAH BAR ASHKĀL-I-UQLAIDIS
Geometry. Period of compilation :— 1332 A.H

54. (XLVII) RISĀLAH MUJADDĪDIN-I-MILLAT
Biography of Reformers.

55. (XLVIII) AL-MU'ALLIFĀT-U-WAL-MU'ALLIFĪN
Biography of writers. Period of compilation :— 1/6/1347 A.H.—1388 A.H.

56. (XLIX) TALKHĪṢ-U-MU'ALLIFĀT WAL-MU'ALLIFĪN
(Summary of the preceding book)

57. (L) ḤAWĀSHĪ UṢŪL-USH-SHĀSHĪ, HIDĀYAH AND OTHER BOOKS Jurisprudence, Sciences of Jurisprudence etc. (Explanatory notes on various books)

URDU WORKS

PUBLISHED

58. (I) KHAṢĀ'IL-i-NABAVĪ SHARḤ-i-SHAMĀ'IL-i-TIRMIDHĪ, Tradition, price : Rs. 6/-, Biography

of the HOLY PROPHET Ṣallallāhu 'Alaihi Wa-Sallam, With Arabic explanatory notes. Period of Compilation :—1343 A.H.—8/6/1344 A.H.

59. (II) TUḤFATUL IKHWĀN Recitation of the Holy QUR'ĀN. (An Urdu translation of the late Qārī Hassan Shā'ir al-Madanī's treatise : Tuḥfatul Ikhwān fī Bayāni-Aḥkām-i-Tajwīd-il Qur'ān Period of compilation :—1345 A.H.—8/5/1345 A.H. (during the author's sojourning in Madinah)

60. (III) FAḌĀ'IL I- QUR'ĀN, Tradition (Virtues of the Holy Qur'an) Price : Re. 0/75 Period of Compilation :— Dhul Hijjah 1348 A H. — 29/12/1348 A.H.

61. (IV) FAḌĀ'IL-i-RAMAḌĀN Tradition, (Virtues of the Fast and the month of Ramaḍān) Price : Re. 0/60 Period of compilation :— Ramaḍān, 1349 A.H.— 27th Ramaḍān, 1349 A.H.

62. (V) FAḌĀ'IL-i-TABLĪGH Tradition, (Virtues of Tablīgh) Price: Re. 0/30 Period of compilation: — 5th Ṣafar, 1350 A.H.—

63. (VI) FADĀ'IL-i-NAMĀZ Tradition (Virtues of Salāt)

Price : Re. 0/80 Date of completion :—7th Muharram, 1358 A.H.

64. (VII) FAḌĀ'IL-i-ḤAJJ Tradition, (Virtues of Pilgrimage) Price : Rs. 3/- Period of compilation 3rd Shawwāl, 1366 A. H.—14/5/1367 A.H.

65. (VIII) FAḌĀ'IL-i-ṢADAQĀT 2 Vols. Price : Rs. 7/- Tradition, (Virtues of Charity) Period of compilation :—1366 A.H. (1947 A.D.)—22/2/1368 A.H.

66. (IX) FAḌĀ'IL-i-DURŪD SHARĪF Tradition, (Virtues of Ṣalawt :— asking Blessings on the Holy Prophet Ṣ A.S) Price : Rs. 1/75 Period of compilation :—25/9/1384 A.H.—6/12/1384 A.H.

67. (X) ḤIKĀYĀT-i-ṢAḤĀBAH History (Stories of the companions of the Holy Prophet Ṣ.A S.) Price : Rs. 2/- Date of completion :— 12/10/1357 A H.

68. (XI) AL I'TIDĀL FĪ MARĀTIBIR-RIJĀL or ISLĀM SIYĀSAT Period of compilation :— 1356 A.H. —29th Sha'bān, 1357 A.H.

69. (XII) RISĀLAH STRIKE Date of completion :— 12th Rabī'ul Awwal, 1388 A.H.

70. (XIII) JUZ'U ASBĀB-i-IKHTILĀF-il-A'IMMAH Causes of difference between the four Imāms. Price : Rs. 1/50

71. (XIV) SĪRAT-i-ṢIDDĪQ Biography of Ḥaḍrat Abū Bakar R A. Published in the monthly Al Siddīq

72. (XV) RISĀLAH ĀP BĪTĪ 5 Vols. (Author's autobiography Period of compilation :—

Vol. I	5/4/1388 A.H.
Vol. II	1390 A.H.
Vol. III	1391 A.H.
Vol IV	1391 A.H.
Vol. V	1391 A.H.

UNPUBLISHED URDU WORKS

73. (1) AL WAQĀI ' WAD-DUHŪR History, Period of compilation :—25/1/1342 A H.—1388 A H.

74. (2) RISĀLAH AL ṬAQDĪR Tradition

75. (3) RISĀLAH FARĀI'Ḍ-I-ḤUSAINĪ **On various subjects**

76. (4) ḤAWĀSHĪ KALĀM-I-PĀK (**in Arabic and Urdu** both) commentary notes on the HOLY QUR'ĀN.

77. (5) MASHĀ'IKH-I-TAṢAWWUF Biography of the Muslim saints.

78. (6) RISĀLAH RADD-I-MAUDŪDIYAT a treatise on Maulana Maudūdi's movement.

79. (7) MASHRIQĪ KĀ ISLĀM a treatise on 'Ināyatullāh Mashriquī

80. (8) MERI MUḤSIN KITĀBAIN (Books from which I benefited myself)

81. (9) NIZĀM-I-MAẒĀHIR 'ULŪM

82. (10) AḤWĀL-MAẒAHIR 'ULŪM (Fifty years survey of the Institution) Period of compilation :— 1335

83. (11) SHARḤI ALFIYAH Grammar. Date of completion :—Thursday 18/8/1329 A.H.

84. (12) SHARḤI SULLAM (Logic)

85. (13) TAQRĪR-I-MISHKĀT Tradition (Lectures on Mishkāt)

86. (14) MAṢHĀIKH -I-CHISHTIYAH (incomplete) Biography of Chishti-saints, period of compilation :- 1335 A H.

TRANSLATIONS IN ENGLISH ETC.

87. (1) VIRTUES OF NAMĀZ : English translation of the Urdu book FAḌĀ 'IL-I-NAMĀZ (S. No. 63 VI) Translations of this book in French and other Indian and foreign languages have also appeared from different parts of the world.

88. (2) VIRTUES OF QUR'ĀN English translation of the Urdu book FADĀ 'IL-i-QUR'ĀN (S. No 60 (III).

89. (3) STORIES OF ṢAḤABAH English translation of the Urdu book ḤĪKĀYĀT-I-ṢAḤĀBAH S. No. 67 (X).

90. (4) MUSLIMS' AFFLICTIONS** (a study of causes and their remedy) ; the book which is in your hand) English translation of the 4th chapter of Urdu book AL I'TIDĀL FĪ MARĀTIB-IR RIJĀL S. No. 68 (XI).

91. (5) ASBĀBU SA'ĀDATIL MUSLIMĪN WA SHAQĀ'HIM Arabic translation of the above S. No. 90 (4).

Note :—There are some other works also.

prepared by :—

11. 12. 1391
28th January, 1972,
Friday

ṢADRUDDĪN 'ĀMIR ANṢĀRI
Muzammil Manzil,
Basti Hazrat Nizamuddin,
New Delhi-13 (INDIA),

**Please see the translator's preface.

بِسْــمِ اللّٰهِ الرَّحْمٰنِ الرَّ حِــيْمِ

(In the name of Allah, the Beneficent, the Merciful)

TRANSLATOR'S PREFACE

The period preceding 1947 was extremely crucial in the history of India, especially for Indian Muslims. It was apparent that the foreign rule was about to end and the British will no longer be the masters of India's destiny. Political leaders were in their high zeal and great spirits. The Muslims were in two main camps. A number of them was demanding partition and almost an equal number was in favour of a united India Both the groups were being supported by 'Ulamās.

The eminent Shaikh of India Ḥaḍrat Maulānā Ḥusain Aḥmed Madanī was among the supporters of United India while the followers of Ḥaḍrat Thānvi were mostly favouring partition. There were meetings after meetings. Numberless articles were published and offensive speeches delivered in support of their respective stands. Processions and slogan-shouting became common feature of every day life. The supporters on either side strongly criticised and condemned the others in public and through papers They would go to the extent of disparaging the 'Ulamās even. They did not mind charging them with innumerable but baseless blames and some times some of them unhesitantly called them names.

In such a humiliating and shabby atmosphere prevalent at that time, Ḥaḍrat Shaikhul Ḥadīth Maulānā Muḥammad Zakariyyā (May he live long !), the author of the book kept him self aloof respecting the 'Ulamās irrespective of their divergent political views. He and his followers would give due regard to the 'Ulamās as usual. A follower-pupil of Ḥaḍrat Shaikhul Ḥadīth at such a confusing and amazing state of affair wrote to him a letter soliciting his enlightened guidance on the following seven items :—

1. Why is there so vast difference of opinion between Ḥaḍrat Thānvī and Ḥaḍrat Madanī though both are most sincere and pious dignitaries ? Do the sincere men of Allah have such astonishing difference ? Is there any justification for that ?

2. Which of the two in your opinion is on the right path ? What do you say about the current issues ?

3. What should we do in the present day circumstances ? Should we commit suicide ? Why don't you come forward and join either side ?

4. The Muslims are speedily going to rack and ruin. What should they do to help themselves out of this difficult situation ?

5. Self-interest rules supreme now-a-days. Each and every one is after his own end.

6. The 'Ulamās are intentionally debased and disparaged. They are unhesitantly abused and charged with impiety.

7. Divergent views of Ulamās are causing great harm to the Ummat.

Hadrat Shaikhul Hadīth replied to him elaborating each item separately in the light of Islamic teachings, the Qur'ānic Commandments and the Traditions. He, however, did not permit it to be published. He allowed only those who were intimate to him to read it personally. It was only at the insistence of Maulānā 'Ābdul Qādir Rāipūrī (Marḥūm) and Maulānā Muḥammad Ilyās Saḥib (Marḥūm) that the Shaikh consented to its publication. Ḥaḍrat Shaikh's book entitled I'tidā or Islāmī Siyāsat is the copy of that letter in print.

The book was readily in great demand and received wide appreciation and great acclaim at the hands of 'Ulamās. The reply in particular to the fourth item worked as an ointment for bruised hearts during the disastrous riots in our country too and its Gujrati translation met with desired results. In view of the paramount importance and proven utility of the book for the anxieties-ridden and afflictions-surrounded Muslims throughout the world, the feeling grew stronger that at least the translation of the fourth item be rendered in different languages. Maulāna Ṣadruddīn 'Amir Anṣāri was successful in persuading me to take up the onerous task of translating it into English. He encouraged and helped me at every step. He went through the manuscript word by word checking all the traditions with the original Arabic texts. It is no exaggeration that he laboured much more than I did in its preparation. Let me admit that it was solely through his valuable guidance and generous co-operation that this small but useful book is in your hands May Allah the Almighty reward him! I am also thankful to Mr. Eḥteshamuddin Qureshi who revised the English text and to Ḥāji Shaikh Ghulām Rasool who rendered his possible help in bringing out the book.

This sort of work is the maiden attempt I have made. I do not claim to be a scholar of English or religious knowledge. My aim is only to perform a humble service of Allah. May He accept it and render it useful ! I would, therefore, request the reader to inform me of my short-comings and to pray for the author, the translator, the revisor, the editor, the publisher and for all those who co-operated in presenting this book to Muslim brothers. May Allah bless us all !

Iftikhar Ahmed Alavi
M. Com., B. Ed.

بِسْمِ اللّٰهِ الرَّحْمٰنِ الرَّحِيْمِ ○

TRANSLATION OF THE 4TH ITEM OF AL—IʻTIDĀL

نَحْمَدُهٗ وَنُصَلِّيْ وَنُسَلِّمُ عَلٰى رَسُوْلِهِ الْكَرِيْمِ

وَعَلٰى اٰلِهٖ وَصَحْبِهٖ وَاَتْبَاعِهِ الْحُمَاةِ لِلدِّيْنِ الْقَوِيْمِ ○

It is true that the Muslims are faced with numerous problems and varied difficulties. Beside individual worries, they are surrounded by troubles and difficulties common for the community. But the question as to what Muslims should do under these circumstances is surprising when it is put by an ordinary sensible Muslim and it is much more astonishing when it comes from an educated one like you. Islam is a perfect religion and Allah the Almighty has declared it complete in His Holy Qur'ān and pronounced that with its completion He has completed His Favours and Grace on man. The Almighty says in such beautiful words :

اَلْيَوْمَ اَكْمَلْتُ لَكُمْ دِيْنَكُمْ وَاَتْمَمْتُ عَلَيْكُمْ نِعْمَتِيْ وَرَضِيْتُ لَكُمُ
الْاِسْلَامَ دِيْنًا ــــــــ (المائدہ، ع ۱)

"This day have I perfected your religion for you (and, with its completion) completed My Favours upon you and have chosen for you Islam as your religion. (I like Islam to be your code of life)"

(Sūrah Māidah, Sec. 1)

What a great honour and how heartening the distinction bestowed on the Muslims is ! Yet the followers of such a perfect religion are perplexed over what they should do. It is too strange. The religion is perfect and there is nothing small or big, worldly or religious that Allah the Almighty and His Holy Prophet Ṣallallāhu 'Alaihi Wa Sallam ! (May Peace be upon him!) have not explained and commanded in clear terms, includin their gains and losses. This explanation is not confined merely to books or oral persuasions but the Holy Prophe Sallallāhu 'Alaihi Wa Sallam ! (May Peace be upon him !) and his dedicated followers have practically proved its practicability and authenticity in their life. To sum up, the good of the world and the Hereafter lies in and depends upon the following of the Holy Prophet Ṣallallāhu 'Alaihi Wa Sallam ! The more sincerely we follow him the more we prosper. But if the following of the Holy Prophet Ṣallallāhu 'Alaihi Wa Sallam ! is deemed to be orthodox and acting upon his ways as shortsightedness, the consequent result, not only that awaits us in the Hereafter is discernable but what follows in this world is also before our own eyes. Every act and word of our beloved Holy Prophet Ṣallallāhu 'Alaihi Wa Sallam ! has been preserved in books by his Companions Raḍiyallāhu 'Anhum ! (May Allah be pleased with them !) and the Muḥadithīn (Traditionists). Let us see how far we follow him. When we compare the present day life of the Ummat (the Muslims) with that of our beloved Holy Prophet Ṣallallāhu 'Alaihi Wa Sallam ! we have to admit that every Sunnat is deliberately and shamelessly discarded. What is worse every Sunnat is being opposed and those who draw attention to it are branded orthodox and foolish. This is an utmost and gruesome cruelty to our own life. Under these circumstances, how Muslims dare complain of their sufferings and hardships and what right they have to cry over them. A Persian poet says :

> There is no way out of our own doings as the ills of life are due to our own ill deeds.

Allah the Almighty has clearly stated :

وَمَآ اَصَابَكُمْ مِّنْ مُّصِيْبَةٍ فَبِمَا كَسَبَتْ اَيْدِيْكُمْ وَيَعْفُوْا عَنْ كَثِيْرٍ ۝ وَ
مَآ اَنْتُمْ بِمُعْجِزِيْنَ فِى الْاَرْضِ ۚ وَمَا لَكُمْ مِّنْ دُوْنِ اللّٰهِ مِنْ وَّلِيٍّ وَّلَا
نَصِيْرٍ ۝ —— (الشورى، ع ۴)

> "Whatever misfortune happens to you, is because of the things your own hands have wrought and (you are not punished for all sins) for many (of them) He grants forgiveness. (If He wills to punish every sin) Nor can ye frustrate Him (aught), (fleeing) through the earth ; nor (will) have ye, besides Allah, any one to protect or to help." (Sūrah Shūrā, Sec. 4)

At another place He says :

> "Mischief (resulting into trials, earthquakes, famine etc.) has appeared on land and sea (everywhere in the world) because of (the deed) that the hands of men have earned, that (Allah) may give them a taste of some of

their deeds ; in order that they turn back (from evil)."

(Sūrah Rūm, Sec. 5)

The above Verses are not the only ones that warn us. The topic referred to above has been discussed and explained hundreds of times in the Holy Qur'ān.

About the first Verse, Ḥaḍrat 'Ali (Raḍiyallāhu 'Anhu !) says. The Holy Prophet Ṣallallāhu 'Alaihi Wa Ṣallam ! told me "I explain to you the meaning of this Verse. O 'Ali, whatever comes to you—a disease, a calamity or any worldly trouble—it is because of the deed that our hands have earned."

Ḥaḍrat Ḥasan says that when this Verse was revealed the Holy Prophet Ṣallallāhu 'Alaihi Wa Sallam ! said : By Him in Whose power lies my life, the scratch of any wood, the stirring of any vein, the stumbling of legs or the striking of a stone from somewhere ; whatever happens there is due to some sin."

Ḥaḍrat Abū Mūsa (Raḍiyallāhu 'Anhu !) quotes the Holy Prophet Ṣallallāhu 'Alaihi Wa Sallam ! said, "Any person who gets a wound or any trouble even less than this, it is because of some ill-doing of his own."

Ḥaḍrat 'Imrān bin Ḥuṣain (Raḍiyāllahu 'Ahnu !) was ill. People came to visit him and felt sorry for his illness. He said: "What is there to feel sorry ? It is because of some sin."

Ḥaḍrat Ḍaḥḥāk says that a person who has learnt the Holy Qur'ān forgets it only due to some sin. He then recited this very Verse and added that there could be no calamity greater than forgetting the Holy Qur'ān.

Ḥaḍrat Asmā, the daughter of Ḥaḍrat Ṣiddīq-i-Akbar Raḍiyallāhu 'Anhu !, once suffered from headache. She put her hand on her head and said that the headache was due to her sins.

This, however, does not mean that sufferings are always due to sins. There are other special causes also. Sometimes the hardships and troubles are caused by reasons other than those discussed above and that for these special causes even the Messengers and innocent children are also put to trials. The details of these reasons and causes are explained at their proper places Here, I don't intend to write a detailed commentary of the Verses and Traditions (Aḥādīth) explaining every aspect. I only mean to emphasise that these Verses and Traditions pronounce as a general rule that the afflictions and sufferings are usually the result of disobedience to Allah. This cause is very often so strong that even those who do not commit such sins are not spared from consequences. So runs a Tradition. The Holy Prophet Ṣallallāhu 'Alaihi Wa Sallam ! said, "In the closing age of this Ummat, there will be Khasf (*i.e.* sinking down of life and houses into the earth), there will be Maskh (metamorphosis *i.e.* changing of men into dogs and monkeys) and there will be Qadhf (*i.e.* raining of stones from the sky)." Some one entreated, "O Holy Prophet Ṣallallāhu 'Alaihi Wa Sallam ! Can we perish even though some pious men are amongst us ?" The Holy Prophet, on whom be the Peace, replied : "Yes, when the vice overcomes good." (Ishā'ah, quoting from Tirmidhī etc.) In fact calamity befalls inspite of the presence of pious men when vice prevails. It has been emphasised in numerous Traditions in various ways to enjoin each other to do good deeds and to forbid from bad ones, otherwise Allah the

Almighty will bring on you some calamity. In some Traditions it has been further stated that even the prayers and supplications at that time will go unheeded.

Another Tradition says, "When some unlawful activity prevails in a certain community and it is within the powers of that community to stop that activity but it does not do so, then Allah the Almighty will send down some calamity on that community before it ceases to exist (in this world)."

To quote one more Tradition, Allah the Almighty once ordered Ḥaḍrat Gabriel to overturn a locality. The angel prayed and said that there was a particular pious man in that locality who had never disobeyed Him. The Almighty replied : "That is right but he never frowned for My sake *i.e.* he felt no sorry even or got angry at the disobedience of people to Me, for this is the least expected of man towards a sin." (Mishkāt)

There are numerous Traditions emphasising this point. It is difficult to reproduce them all here. They state that the least expected of men is to feel sorry on seeing wrong deeds if stopping of such deeds is beyond their control ; if it is not done, the Torment of Allah may come down. Now let us assess our own condition in the light of the above warnings. We commit sins every moment, and according to the Verses and Traditions referred to above we deserve much more punishment. We must have been put to multitude sufferings and troubles because of our wrong doings. In addition to our own sins, we feel no grief or anxiety over the prevailing disobedience to Allah ; the sins are being constantly committed before our own eyes and we never feel aggrieved on this plight. In such circumstances, what hope we can have of our prayers and supplications being granted and how our troubles and sufferings can be remedied But for the Mercy of Allah and the accepted prayers of the Holy Prophet and that we fortunately happen to be his Ummat, all of us must have been destroyed. Our relation, though the weakest, with the Holy Prophet Ṣallallāhu 'Alaihi Wa Sallam ! saves us from annihilation. Ours is a condition where every sin is a matter of pride and every sort of apostasy a sure way to success. Any one speaking renegade language is considered progressive and if some one wishes or dares object him, he is branded as Kat Mullā and is said to be liable to be slain. Such a man is said not to know anything of the world or understand the need of the hour ; an enemy of progress and a hurdle to development.

It was a general view of Divine Commandments and our adherence to them. Turning to details, let us take a few examples.

The most important Ordain of Islam, next to Īmān (Faith) is Ṣalāt *i e.* Daily Prayers. The numerous Traditions state that discarding (non-performance) of Ṣalāt causes Rejection of Faith. The very distinctive feature that separates a Muslim from an Unbeliever (Kāfir) is Ṣalāt. There are numberless losses a man might suffer in the Hereafter as well as in this life, due to his discarding Ṣalāt. I have briefly explained them in my booklet "Faḍāi'l-i-Namāz" (*i e.* Virtues of Salāt)[1]. I need not repeat them here. But how many Muslims are there who are particular about the performance of this important duty. Moreover, it is a pity that no one dares point it out to those who do not perform Ṣalāt. A poor Muslim may be reproached on his neglecting Ṣalāt but none dares to do so against a well-

1. This book is available in Urdu, English and French.

to-do person. A rich man or one who enjoys some sort of power or authority is not reprimanded. None dares approach an influential person in society to remind him of this duty. The situation is still worse ; the malady has gone deeper and a person publicly announces that Ṣalāt is not a Divine Worship and such a person, what to object or reproach him, is praised and called 'Allāma (Scholar). He is credited with understanding the need of the hour. He is commended as a well-wisher of Muslims and is deemed to be well aware of the required remedy. Any one speaking against him is called illiterate and Imām of Two Rak'ats only, and ignorant of the call of the time and necessities of the Muslims. They altogether forget that Ṣalāt is the coolness of eyes of the Holy Prophet Ṣallallāhu 'Alaihi Wa Sallam ! Alas ! One who claims to be the follower of the Holy Prophet Ṣallallāhu 'Alaihi Wa Sallam ! and yet declares Ṣalāt to be a useless duty and thereupon earns the title of farsightedness and deep thinking. With such a dreadful plight, what right the Muslims have to complain of sufferings and afflictions. In such circumstances and with so many wrong deeds on our part, we actually deserve much more punishment than what we receive and this is but due to Allah's Kindness, Tolerance and Mercy that we are not yet defaced from this world.

It was only as regards one tenet of Islam. As to other tenets of Islam like Fasting in Ramaḍān, Zakāt or Ḥajj, a glance on the whole world sufficiently shows our indifference. How many of us observe them in real spirit ! On the contrary, we shamelessly indulge in all taboos. Drinking of wine is, for instance, quite common. You will see that the persons who claim to be the devotees of Islam and to be ever-ready-to-die for its cause, are addicted to liquor and they drink it openly and imprudently. The Holy Qur'ān repeatedly warns against all transactions of wine and has forbidden it in clear words. The Holy Prophet Ṣallallāhu 'Alaihi Wa Sallam! has cursed those who drink it, who prepare it or get it prepared, who buy and sell it, who carry it and those to whom it is carried, who serve it and those who use the sale proceeds of it. Another Tradition states. The Holy Prophet said : "Ḥaḍrat Gabriel came to me and said, "O Muḥammad (On whom be the Peace), verily Allah the Almighty has cursed wine, He has cursed one who prepares and gets it prepared, one who drinks it or carries it and one to whom it is carried, its seller and server and one who gets it served (*i.e.* a master who gets it served through his servant or subordinate, then the servant becomes the server and the master is one who gets it served)." Hākim testifies both these Traditions as Ṣaḥīḥ.

Now, it is for us to think that due to only one single act of drinking, how many persons are liable to the curse of Allah the Almighty and the Holy Prophet Ṣallallāhu 'Alaihi Wa Sallam ! (May Allah save us all !). What would be the fate of those who are cursed by Allah the Almighty and His Prophet Ṣallallāhu 'Alaihi Wa Sallam ! who has been extremely kind to his followers and always thought of the betterment and success of his Ummat. And what would be the fate of those who do not prevent or reproach the drinker, inspite of their capability to do so. Think of your own condition. If some one dares reprimand or object, he is deemed to be shortsighted and a toy-scholar. The Holy Prophet Ṣallallāhu 'Alaihi Wa Sallam ! said, "Abstain from wine. It is the root of every sin."

When we ourselves unlock the flood gate of the afflictions,

why to complain of when they overcome us. Can there be any limit to this foolishness that despite warnings by our Holy Prophet Ṣallallāhu 'Alahi Wa Sallam ! that the troubles and hardships follow evils, we keep on committing them.

Likewise, take the case of Ribā (usury). First, ponder over the Commandments of Allah and His Holy Prophet Ṣallallāhu 'Alaihi Wa Sallam ! and think how emphatically Allah the Almighty has forbidden Ribā (usury) in His Holy Book Allah from His side and from the side of His Holy Prophet Sallallāhu 'Alaihi Wa Sallam ! has declared war against those who do not abstain from usury. So says Allah :

﴿فَإِن لَّمْ تَفْعَلُوا فَأْذَنُوا بِحَرْبٍ مِّنَ اللَّهِ وَرَسُولِهِ﴾ (البقرة، ع ٣٨)

"(O ye who believe, fear Allah and give what remains of your demand for usury, if ye are indeed believers). If you do it not, take notice of war from Allah and His Apostle."
(Sūrah Baqarah, Sec. 38)

As in the days of ignorance and illiteracy, transactions involving interest were quite common, the above Commandment was revealed forbidding money-lenders from accepting even the interest due at that time. There was no question of entering into any new transactions of this sort. There have been numerous warnings in Traditions against usury transactions. A number of Traditions conclude that the graveness of the sin of usury may be divided into seventy three stages and the least of all is equal to fornication with his mother and the worst degree is like disgracing (humiliating) a Muslim.

A Tradition states : "Save yourself from such sins as would not be pardoned and (taking of) interest is one of them.

Any one who charges interest will be resurrected like an insane on the Day of Judgment."

At one time, the Holy Prophet Ṣallallāhu 'Alaihi Wa Sallam ! said, "One who is brought up on income from interest will not enter the Paradise." (Mishkāt)

The Holy Prophet Ṣallallāhu 'Alaihi Wa Sallam ! in various Traditions has cursed one who charges interest, who pays interest, who is wintness to such a transaction, and one who writes a deed relating to interest. What a bad luck is he going to meet whom the Holy Prophet Ṣallallāhu 'Alaihi Wa Sallam ! curses!

A Tradition states, "Any nation wherein adultery and usury become common in practice, that nation has prepared for itself the anguish (Torture) of Allah."

Keeping in view the above warnings, just assess the present-day circumstances in terms of Divine Precepts. Numberless dealings involve interest openly. What is more, such transactions are deemed (divinely) lawful and booklets are written to establish lawfulness of interest. Any one speaking against it is opposed, and accused of baseless charges, and efforts are made that no one listens to him.

I have briefly stated the above examples. As to the other Commandments, you just see and think over. There is indifference and negligence towards and even refusal to almost all Commandments that are to be observed. The Commandments forbidding us from sins are declared unlawful and undivine and the sins are openly and shamelessly practised. There is none to oppose or forbid such people and if there happens to be some one, he is called conservative-minded and his condition is qu ite clear.

Having cited the above examples, I would better quote a few Traditions to elucidate that our sufferings and troubles are of our own making and there is none to blame but ourselves.

When the Muslims believe the Holy Prophet Ṣallallāhu 'Alaihi Wa Sallam ! to be the righteous and true, they must believe that the hardships and troubles that he has stated to be the sequel of the particular actions and deeds are bound to result, and if we want to escape from them, then we must abandon those activities and deeds. We jump into the fire and shout that we are burnt. It is of no use. Study these Traditions carefully and repeatedly.

The Holy Prophet Ṣallallāhu 'Alihi Wa Ṣallam ! states, "My Ummat will be doomed to hardships and sufferings when it takes to the following 15 misdeeds :—

1. Booty becomes one's own property.
2. Deposit is treated as booty.
3. Payment of Zakāt is deemed to be penalty.

4&5. Obedience to wife and disobedience to mother prevails.

6&7. Good treatment towards friends and acquaintances and cruel behaviour with father gets in vogue.

8. There is hue and cry in mosques.
9. Mean persons become responsible ones of the community.
10. A person is respected only to be safe from his wickedness (*i.e.* the man is not by himself respectable but he is respected only because he will put us in dfficulty if we do not show him respect).

11. Drinking of wine.
12. Wearing of silken dress (by males).
13. Dancing girls are sponsored.
14. Musical instruments are manufactured (for wider use).
15. People appearing in the latter ages of this Ummat repudiate the people of the earlier period.

At this stage the people consequently should wait for (such torments as) red hurricanes, sinking into the earth and metamorphosis."

Another Tradition states, "When Baitul-Māl (public treasury) is treated as the personal property and the deposit is considered as booty and the Zakāt is deemed to be a penalty tax and (religious) knowledge is attained for purposes other than those of religion (i.e. for worldly ends like wealth and property and glory); submission to wife and disobedience to mother prevails; closeness to acquaintances and turning away from father becomes common; there is hue and cry in mosques and debauchees become leaders; mean people hold authority; man is respected for fear of his wickedness; singing girls and musical instruments become quite common; wines are drunk and the early people of the Ummat are disparaged; then, at that time, they should expect for red hurricane, earthquake. sinking down into the earth and metamorphosis and raining of stones from the sky."

Almost exactly the same subject, as in the above two Traditions. is stated in a third Tradition with the addition that (when) the young chaps (unmatured) preach from the pulpits. Is there any one of these affairs that the Holy Prophet Ṣallallāhu 'Alaihi Wa Sallam! has ennumerated in the Traditions which is not excessively practised? Take these sins one by one.

A look at the world conditions will assure you that the whole world is involved in it.

Hadrat 'Abdullah bin 'Abbas says, "A community wherein dishonesty is prevalent, Allah the Almighty will create fear of the enemy in the hearts of the people of that community and a community wherein fornication is widely practised, there will be excess of deaths in that community. Any community that adopts under-weighing and under-measuring, its provision will be reduced; the community that departs from justice (passes against what is right) will suffer from killings and murders, and the people who break promises, Allah will impose on them some enemy. (Mishkāt)

Hadrat Ibn 'Umar (Raḍiyallāhu 'Anhu!) narrates that the Holy Prophet Ṣallallāhu 'Alaihi Wa Sallam! once paid special attention and emphatically said, "O, the group (community) of Muhājireen (Migrants)! There are five such things if, Allah forbids, you are involved in them (their torments will be brought on you): A community wherein fornication prevails will be exposed to plague and diseases new and unheard of before; the community that adopts under-weighing and under-measuring will suffer from famines, hardships and the tyrannies of the king; and the people withholding Zakāt will have no rain. If there were no animals, there will not be (a single drop of rain (i.e. the little rain that falls on the community will come only for the sake of animals); and the people who break the covenant of Allah and His Holy Prophet Ṣallallāhu 'Alaihi Wa Sallam! they will be surrounded by enemies and those who take to injustice will be involved in civil war." (Targhīb)

The warning that the spread of fornication causes poverty has been stated innumerable times. The Holy Prophet Ṣallallāhu 'Alaihi Wa Sallam! is reported to have said, "A community that breaks the covenant will be exposed to blood-shed ; the community wherein fornication spreads will suffer excessive deaths ; the community withholding Zakāt will be deprived of rain." It is stated in a Tradition that the people among whom bribery becomes common, tneir hearts will be overawed (by one and all). Ḥaḍrat Ka'ab says that the destruction of this Ummat will be due to the breach of covenant. (Durr-i-Manthūr)

The Holy Prophet Ṣallallāhu 'Alaihi Wa Sallam! is reported to have said, "There will be a group of persons in this Ummat that will be busy with eating and amusement at night and will be changed by the morning into apes and hogs and some of them will meet the Wrath of Allah through sinking down into the earth. People will shout the next day : Tonight has sunk such and such family and house. Some people will be stoned from the sky like the people of Lot and some others will be washed away by the dust storms. And all these misfortunes will be the consequences of their drinking wine, wearing silken dress, keeping dancing girls, practising usury and disregard of cogational relationships." (Ḥākim describes this Tradition as Ṣaḥīḥ--Durr-i-Manthūr)

A Tradition explains that the duty the observance of which brings the quickest future reward is the regard of cogational relationship. It happens that some family members commit sins yet they continue to be blessed with prosperity in their progeny as well as in their wealth only because they regard cogational relationship. In contrast to this, the cruelty and false oaths are sins that bring down the Wrath of Allah the Almighty quicker than any other sin and these sins cause destruction of property, sterilisation of women and excessive death i.e. there are a lot of deaths. (Durr-i-Manthūr) The Holy Prophet Ṣallallāhu 'Alaihi Wa Sallam! says, "Allah Ta'ālā defers the consequences of sins for any time He likes save the disobedience to parents ; the consequences thereof have to be borne in this very life before death." (Durr) Says the Holy Prophet Ṣallaliāhu 'Alaihi Wa Sallam! "Be chaste so that your wives too may remain chaste. Behave kindly with your parents so that your children too behave with you the same way." (Durr)

The Holy Prohphet Ṣallallāhu 'Alaihi Wa Sallam! emphatically states, "By Allah in Whose possession my life lies, enjoin upon people to do good deeds and forbid from bad deeds, otherwise Allah the Almighty will bring on you some calamity and any prayers and supplications at that time will go unheeded." Another Tradition states, "Keep on ordering people to do what is right and forbidding them from what is wrong before such a time comes when your prayers will not be granted." It is stated in a Tradition, "Allah does not bring down a common calamity due to unlawful deeds of certain people unless the deeds are committed before the people who have power to stop but never do so and when such a state arrives, the calamity befalls all, ordinary or privileged." (Durr)

These are the causes due to which new sorts of calamities, earthquakes, storms, famines, collision of trains etc. have become a common feature of today. Diseases and disasters of new varieties are on the increase which never occurred before. People habitual of reading newspapers know it very well. As the practice of enjoining what is right and forbidding from what is wrong is almost nil, there is therefore hardly any hope of our prayers being granted. What it may gain us only to announce for prayers and supplications after Ṣalāt when we ourselves adopt such means as cause rejection of prayers.

In many Traditions the Holy Prophet Ṣallallāhu 'Alaihi

Wa Sallam! is reported to have cursed those who offer and accept bribe. Some Traditions also include in curse the third person who acts as mediator between the briber and the bribee. Now see how many people are indulged in this sin and what will be their fate when Allah the Almighty and His Holy Prophet Ṣallallāhu 'Alaihi Wa Sallam! curse them. The Holy Prophet Ṣallallāhu 'Alaihi Wa Sallam! is stated to have said in a Tradition, "Don't be oppressor, otherwise your prayers will not be granted." In another Tradition it is stated, "Allah the Almighty respites the oppresssor. (Perhaps he may refrain from it). But once He takes them to task, they cannot escape." Allah the Almighty says :

وَكَذٰلِكَ اَخْذُ رَبِّكَ اِذَآ اَخَذَ الْقُرٰى وَهِىَ ظَالِمَةٌ اِنَّ اَخْذَهٗٓ اَلِيْمٌ

شَدِيْدٌ — (هود: ع ٩)

"Your Allah's grip is strong. When He catches hold of the residents of a locality who are cruel, His grip is surely too much painful and strong." (Sūrah Hūd, Sec. 9)

Now look at the tyrannies prevailing in the world and think for a while what limit can be there to the sufferings and troubles when Allah the Almighty Himself calls to account. A Tradition states that the oppressed's call is readily granted, be he a dissolute. Another Tradition says that be he an Unbeliever. (Targhīb & Hisn-i-Ḥaṣīn)

In a Tradition Allah the Almighty says, "I am extremely angry with the person who does injustice with a person who keeps none but Me as his Helper." A Persian poet says meaning thereby : Be on the watch against the call of the oppressed, for the Divine Acceptance itself comes down to embrace the call of the oppressed.

The Holy Prophet Ṣallallāhu 'Alaihi Wa Sallam! says,

"Those in the sky do not sympathise with those who are not kind towards people on the earth." (Targhīb)

In these circumstances when the curses of the oppressed are on the increase every day and those in the sky show no kindness, it is easily understandable how many thunderbolts, hails and storms are likely to befall and to what extent. It is reported in a Tradition, "Save yourself from the curse of the oppressed as there is no hindrance in the acceptance of his call, be he a debauchee or a dissolute fellow." A Tradition reports Allah the Almighty to have said, "I never neglect the suppplication of the oppressed, be he an Unbeliever." (Ḥaṣīn) It is stated in a Tradition, "My Ummat will be on the path of welfare till illegitimate children are not born in abundance and when it so happens, Allah the Almighty will inflict some encompassing penalty on that Ummat." (Targhīb)

What to speak of secret adultery, is there any city, big or small, wherein prostitution is not practised in public and where birth of unlawful children is not very common. Muslim members of Municipal Corporations are campelled to arrange for permanent centres of these ever-on-the-increase illegitimate (fatherless) children and to arrange for vast areas to house them. The Holy Prophet Ṣallallāhu 'Alaihi Wa Sallam! says, "In any locality where usury and adultery spreads, let the people of that locality know that they are throwing themselves to the Wrath of Allah the Almighty." Just think over it and see how many persons are indulged in this shameful sin and how many so-called cultured and civilized men are letting houses for such a dreadful sin and how many religious Municipal Commissioners are compelled to arrange shelters for such a mean act.

A number of Traditions report, "The angels (of Benevolence) do not enter that house where there is a dog or a picture." Abu Wāil (Raḍiyallāhu 'Anhu!) narrates, "I took part in a battle of Syria in the company of Ḥaḍrat 'Umar (Raḍiyallāhu 'Anhu!). We happened to stay at a place. A noble man of that place came searching (keenly desirous of visiting) Ḥaḍrat 'Umar (Raḍiyallāhu 'Anhu!). Approaching Ḥaḍrat 'Umar (Raḍiyallāhu 'Anhu!)' he prostrated before him. Ḥaḍrat 'Umar (Raḍiyallāhu 'Anhu!) enquired what it was. He replied that it was their normal custom to do before kings. Ḥaḍrat 'Umar (Raḍiyallāhu 'Anhu!) exhorted : Prostrate only before Allah the Almighty Who created you. Then the noble said, 'I have arranged a feast for you. I implore you to come to my house and dine with me.' Ḥaḍrat 'Umar (Raḍiyallāhu 'Anhu!) asked him if there were any pictures in his house. When the noble replied in the affirmative, Ḥaḍrat 'Umar (Raḍiyallāhu 'Anhu!) declined to go there and asked to send to him only one type of food. The noble sent it and Ḥaḍrat 'Umar (Raḍiyallāhu 'Anhu!) took it." (Hākim)

Now, have a look at the civilized houses of today. Can there be any decoration without pictures and can any Maulvī dare object to it? Tell me how can the ever-increasing afflictions of Muslims be decreased when we ourselves close the doors to Allah's Benevolence and adopt all possible means which cause Allah's Wrath. It is but natural that under these circumstances there should be every moment an increase in our troubles and sufferings. Our ancestors' behaviour was such that they would not like to go even to the house of Unbelievers where there were pictures and we the disobedient descendants who claim to be Muslims decorate with our own hands our houses with these unlawful items. Just ponder over the sayings of the Holy Prophet Ṣallallāhu 'Alaihi Wa Sallam! and assess yourself and the world. The perfectness of Islam's teachings and the detraction of Muslims from religious education is a very amazing phenomenon. The Holy Prophet Ṣallallāhu 'Alaihi Wa Sallam! says, "When the sun rises, two angels standing close to it announce : O people ! Be attentive to your Allah. A little of provision that suffices (your needs) is better than the heap of wealth which engages you in lavish amusement. And when the sun sets in, two angels standing near it pray : "O Allah ! Recompense one who spends (in the right way) and destroy the goods of one who keeps in store." (Targhīb)

Now think what a dreadful plight awaits those who store wealth. They tolerate a lot of sufferings in its collection and when their miserliness does not allow them to spend it in the Way of Allah, they invite multifarious sufferings to destroy it. Sometimes they fall ill and hundreds of rupees are lost by way of medical bill, sometimes they get involved in some litigation, right or wrong, which ultimately dissolves the whole of their property and if some people's property is safe by virtue of their certain good deed, their successors get so astray that they indulge in lavish amusements and spend off in months that which their predecessors had collected over numerous years. These are not imaginary tales but are based on day-to-day real facts. We see that huge wealth collected by their elders with the sweat of brow is spent lavishly within a few weeks of their death by their successors. Hence, numerous Traditions state, "Man shouts : This property is mine, that property is mine ! But in fact his property is only that much that he eats or wears or deposits with Allah the Almighty (by spending in the Way of Allah). Other than that belongs to others." (Targhīb)

Haḍrat 'Alī (Raḍiyallāhu 'Anhu!) says, "Whatever you store more than that you require for maintenance belongs to others and you are the keeper of that." (Kitābu-l-Mukhallāt)

Hundreds of Traditions state that anything in excess of personal needs is meant not for collection but for spending on others. The Holy Qur'ān says:

يَسْـَٔلُوْنَكَ مَاذَا يُنْفِقُوْنَ قُلِ الْعَفْوَ ــــــ (البقرۃ، ع ٢٧)

"They ask thee how much they are to spend ; Say : What is beyond your needs (that it is easy to spare)."

(Sūrah Baqarah, Sec. 27)

Ḥaḍrat Ibn 'Abbās (Raḍiyallāhu 'Anhu!) states "Beyond your needs" means what is left out on meeting the family needs. Here let us consider another point i.e. the subject of helping the poor and eradicating poverty. It is these days given great importance but can there be any remedy better than what is contained in the Islamic teachings. Forcing one not to get more than what is required and persuading one not to keep any thing beyond one's needs and spending all with strong desire and full assent on the poor. Their is a world of difference in the two views. The first view is sheer cruelty and the other one mere goodness. The first one discourages ambitions and makes the spirited people idle whereas the other one encourages the spirits and prepares people to earn more than what they do and to spend it happily. Moreover, man is encouraged in the Islamic teachings not only on ,spending what is beyond their needs but also on killing their needs to spend on others. Hence, the Holy Qur'ān while praising the Anṣārs states :

يُؤْثِرُوْنَ عَلٰٓى اَنْفُسِهِمْ وَلَوْ كَانَ بِهِمْ خَصَاصَةٌ قف ــــ (الحشر، ع ١)

"They give them (i.e. the Muhājirīn) preference over themselves, even though poverty was their lot." (Sūrah Ḥashr, Sec. 1)

And all this what we have been reading are not oral utterings but the Holy Prophet Ṣallallāhu 'Alaihi Wa Sallam! showed it by practising himself and getting it practised by others. The whole of life of the Holy Prophet Ṣallallāhu 'Alaihi Wa Sallam! and the life of his companions Raḍiyallāhu 'Anhum! are a witness to it. The chapters of the Tradition books "Az-Zuhad" and "Ar-Riqāq" are full of these topics and for a glimpse of such characters, have a look at the Ḥikayāt-i-Ṣaḥābah (Stories of the Companions Raḍiyallāhu 'Anhum!) wherein I have quoted some examples. Here, neither the topic demands nor the space permits of this discussion. What I wish to say is that the sort of troubles we are surrounded by are of our own and a doctor, righteous, reliable and perfect, whose prescription never fails nor is there such a possibility, has clearly brought out the causes of diseases and has also prescribed the treatment. Now, it is not for the doctor to escape from the causes and to go under treatment. It is the duty of the patient to do so. If some one does not care, he himself exposes to loss. The Holy Prophet Ṣallallāhu 'Alaihi Wa Sallam! states, "Verily I have brought to you such a Sharī'at (Law) which is clear and bright." At another place he says, "By Allah, I have left you on such (a way) that is (brightly) white and its day and night are equal." The Holy Prophet Ṣallallāhu 'Alaihi Wa Sallam! has warned against each and every thing and within his short span of life he has left no part of the religion or the world unreviewed. The Holy Prophet Ṣallallāhu 'Alaihi Wa Sallam! states, "Make haste in performing (good) deeds and (perform them) before such trials appear which will be like the parts of dark night (when any distinction between right and wrong is rather difficult) wherein a man will be Mūmin in the morning and Kāfir (Unbeliever) in the evening; Mūmin in the evening and Kāfir in the morning; he will sell his religion for a few pieces of the world." (Targhīb) The Holy Prophet Ṣallallāhu 'Alaihi Wa

Sallam! says, "Turn to (and seek forgiveness of) Allah before you are dead; do good deed before you are envisaged by concerns; establish contact with Allah the Almighty by remembering Him too often and by giving alms secretly or openly; for these deeds you will be rewarded with provision, you will be assisted and your loss too will be made up." (Targhīb)

A Tradition says, "Property does not decrease by giving alms; whosoever pardons the tyrant, Allah adds to his honour; so always pardon the tyrant and Allah will reward you with honour; any person who takes to begging is doomed to poverty." (Mu'jam Saghīr) Another Tradition runs like this, "When my Ummat has animosity with its (religious) scholars, decoration of bazaars gets prominence and marriages are done only for wealth (i.e. consideration for marriage is wealth rather than nobility), then Allah the Almighty will bring on four things : famine, the ruler's tyranny, officials' embezzlement and enemy's invasion." (Ḥākim) Ḥaḍrat 'Ali (Raḍiyallāhu 'Anhu!) says, "The laziness in offering prayers, the reduction of maintenance and happiness, come as punishment for sins." (Tārīkhul-Khulafā) Ḥaḍrat Anas (Raḍiyallāhu 'Anhu!) says, "I served the Holy Prophet Ṣallallāhu 'Alaihi Wa Sallam! for ten years but he never talked to me surly. He exhorted me : Make Wuḍū properly because it increases age and the guarding angels will begin to love you." (Ṭabrānī Ṣaghīr) "And perform part of your prayers at home as it would add to the blessings of your house. And when you enter your house, say 'Salām' to your family members, its blessings will be bestowed on you as well as your family members."

A glimpse of the blessings worldly or religious which the Holy Prophet Ṣallallāhu 'Alaihi Wa Sallam! has explained on Ṣalāt can be seen in my booklet "The Virtues of Ṣalāt". I don't want to mention those virtues and blessings here for reasons of brevity. All these statements amply explain that as excessive sins and wrong deeds cause excessive troubles and sufferings, similarly obedience and prayers result in the good of the worlds. Says the Holy Prophet Ṣallallāhu 'Alaihi Wa Sallam! :

إن الله تعالى يقول يا ابن آدم تفرّغ لعبادتي أملأ صدرك غنى
وأسد فقرك وإن لا تفعل ملأت يدك شغلا ولم أسد فقرك، كذا
في الجامع الصغير برواية أحمد والترمذي وابن ماجة والحاكم
عن أبي هريرة ورقم له بالحسن ٥

Allah the Almighty says, "O, the descendants of Adam!. You devote time for My worship, I shall fill your heart with peace (and satisfaction) and do away with your poverty (and starvation) and if you don't do so (i.e. devote yourself for My prayers), I shall fill your heart with concerns and worries and will not reduce your poverty."

This is the declaration of Allah, All-Powerful, Owner of the worlds in Whose possession every thing of the two worlds is. Also there are many other statements having the same theme and wherein the success of the world is said to depend solely on Allah's worship. But we people first of all forget our prayers and get lost in earning the livelihood or worldly comfort. We sacrifice former for the latter. When we think in this way that our success lies in disobedience to Allah the Almighty, then why there should not be an increase in our troubles and sufferings. Neglecting the religion, the Muslims wish to solve the problems of bread. How is it possible when the Bread-giver Himself states that He would not do away with poverty, nor would He free heart from anxieties and worries if we do not obey Him. It is reported in a Ṣaḥīḥ Tradition that Allah the Almighty says, "If the people obey My Commandments (in all respects), I will bring rain on them at night when they are sleeping and make the sun shine throughout the day (so that their business is not interrupted) and they don't even hear any thunder clap (so that they know no fear)." (Jāmi'ul Ṣaghīr) But see our ill-luck ! What to speak of such an organised system of day and night, our complaints about droughts are ever-increasing and where there are rains, they are usually followed by floods.

It is narrated in the Iḥyā of Imām Ghazālī : Once there was acute famine during the days of Ḥaḍrat Moses (May Peace be upon him!). Ḥaḍrat Moses 'Alaihi-Assalām would go out on three days along with Bani Israel to offer Ṣalāt-i-Istisqā but it would not rain. The third day it was revealed to him that there was a back-biter in his party and because of his presence amongst them that their prayers were not granted. Ḥaḍrat Moses 'Alaihi-Assalām begged Allah the Almighty to identify that man so that he could be excluded from the party. Allah's reply was . When I forbid you from back-biting, how I Myself can spy that man and therefore I do not name that fellow. Ḥaḍrat Moses 'Alaihi-Assalām thereupon addressed his people and advised them to turn to Allah and ask His Forgiveness. When Ḥaḍrat Moses 'Alaihi-Assalām made them vow not to commit sin particularly back-biting, it soon rained. Ḥaḍrat Sufyān Thaurī (Raḥmatullāh 'Alaihi) is quoted to have said : In Bani Israel there was such an acute famine for seven years that people started eating even the corpses from the heap shells, so much so they took to man-eating. The distressed people in their utter miserable condition would every day go to mountains and forests for prayers and Ṣalāt-i-Istisqā. Allah the Almighty revealed to the Messengers of that time : Howsoever your tongues are dried in offering prayers and your hands for prayers may rise even up to the sky, I shall not pity for any weeper till the tyrannies prevailing amongst you are done away with.

Books on History and Traditions are full of such incidents. In short, there are hundreds of statements which explicitly detail that the successes of both the worlds depend upon good deeds and that the losses of the two worlds result from bad deeds. It is neither my aim nor is it possible to discuss all such statements here. The purpose of referring to such incidents is only to stress that if we consider the statements of the Holy Prophet Ṣallallāhu 'Alaihi Wa Sallam! to be true, then how much explicit cruelty we commit ourselves by falling prey to these pernicious sins. It is of no use shouting out the elegy of Muslims' destruction and to keep on inviting destruction. Our example is like that of a patient who suffers from diarrhoea but constantly takes purgative medicines and loudly complains against having loose bowels. Some one should ask that fool that when he himself continues to take purgative medicines, how can he hope to cure diarrhoea. We always complain about the tyrannies of the British rule and are much afraid of the successor government. But has not the Holy Prophet Ṣallallāhu 'Alaihi Wa Sallam! warned us against such odds? Has he not clearly explained: kinds of governments are a direct result of our deeds? Is there any deficiency in the teachings of the Holy Prophet Ṣallallāhu 'Alaihi Wa Sallam! and his affection to us? Nay, every thing is complete and clear. The Holy Prophet Ṣallallāhu 'Alaihi Wa Sallam! (May my soul, my father and my mother be sacrificed for him!) says : As you be (in your deeds) so will the rulers be imposed on you. (Mishkāt) Hence, if we desire to be ruled by the best and the choicest people, the only remedy for that are our best deeds and nothing else. In another Tradition the Holy Prophet Ṣallallāhu 'Alaihi Wa Sallam! states: Allah the Almighty says, "I am Allah. There is no God save Me. I am the Master and King of all kings. I hold the hearts of kings in My Hand. When people obey Me, I turn the hearts of kings towards kindness and mercy on them. When they disobey Me, I turn the hearts of kings for anger and revenge on them and thereby they put them to wrath (and sufferings). Hence, instead of cursing the kings turn towards My Remembrance and implore (of Me) so that I guard you against their tyrannies. Mālik Ibn Maghool says that he has read the same topic in Hadrat Dawood ('Alaihi-Assalam)'s Zabūr.

Such topics have been repeatedly quoted in several Traditions. The Traditional prayer states:

O Allah! We implore you not to impose on us, due to our sins, such persons who would not be kind to us.

Allah the Almighty says:

وَكَذٰلِكَ نُوَلِّي بَعْضَ الظّٰلِمِينَ بَعْضًا بِمَا كَانُوا يَكْسِبُونَ ۝ — (الانعام ع ١٥)

"Thus do We make the wrong-doers turn to each other because of what they earn." (Surah An'ām, Sec. 15)

Various explanations have been given to this Verse. The author of Jalālain has adopted the very explanation i.e. cruel persons on account of their bad deeds will be ruled over by tyrants. Hadrat Qatāda (Radiyallāhu 'Anhu) says: It is cruel Jins who are imposed on cruel persons. And A'mash says : When people's deeds go wrong, the wrost people are made their rulers.

Hadrat 'Umar (Raḍiyallāhu 'Anhu) says : It is narrated to me that Ḥaḍrat Christ ('Alaihi-Assalam) or Hadrat Moses ('Alaihi

Assalam, enquired of Allah the Almighty what the sign of His being happy with the people was. Allah Ta'ālā's reply was : I send rain to them at the time of sowing the fields and stop it at the time of harvest. Their administrative affairs are entrusted to the courteous and polite people and the common property is put under the supervision of honest people. He enquired what the sign of His being angry with the people was. The answer to it was: I stop rain during the sowing season and pour it down during the harvesting time. Their administrative responsibilities are entrusted to fools and the common property is under the supervision of the niggards. (Dur)

The Holy Prophet Ṣallallāhu 'Alaihi Wa Sallam! states, "Always enjoin what is right and forbid what is wrong, otherwise Allah the Almighty will appoint the worst people as your rulers. Then, any prayers and supplications even by the best people among you will not be granted." (Jāmi')

There are people who fail to understand why the prayers of pious persons are not granted or why they do not pray at all. Let them think over it for a while that how much they enjoin upon people to do what is right and forbid what is wrong. When such practice is no more there, how can there be any hope of prayers being granted. It is stated in a Tradition, "When Allah the Almighty intends betterment of any community, He appoints magnanimous people as rulers (who do not outrage) and religious scholars decide their issues (in the light of knowledge they take the right and just decisions on the basis of merit of cases) and generous people are entrusted with the property (so that every person is benefited by their generosity). When some community (for its wrong deeds) is reproached, the stupid are made rulers and illiterate become judges and property is in the custody of misers."

Another Tradition says: When Allah the Almighty is angry with any community and does not inflict His extreme Wrath in the form of sinking or defacing, then He raises prices, stops rain and imposes the worst people as rulers. In another Tradition Allah the Almighty is reported to have said : I take revenge through such persons whose portion is My Wrath (i.e. with whom I am angry) from those other persons whose portion is My Wrath. (I detail one cruel to oppress other cruel) And then I throw them all to Hell. That is why, it is stated in a Tradition : Never abuse the rulers, Pray for their capability and goodness because in their capability lies your goodness (i.e. abusing will not make them mend their ways).

Another Tradition says: Don't engage your hearts in abusing kings and emperors but solicit nearness to Allah the Almighty and pray attentively to Him to make their hearts kind towards you.

Makki Bin Ibrahim says, "We were sitting in the company of Ibne 'Aun. People started talking of Bilāl bin Abī Bardah and abused him. Ibne 'Aun remained silent. People told him that they abused Bilāl only because of him, for he was cruel to him. Ibne 'Aun retorted: Every word is recorded in my Character Roll (Book of deeds) and it will be read out on the Day of Judgment. I very much wish that there is as much of La Ilāha Illallāh as possible instead of accusations on anyone. (Iḥyā) Once some one in the presence of a pious man cursed the cruel Ḥajjāj. The pious man exhorted: Don't curse. Whatever is there, it is due to your own deeds. I fear if Ḥajjāj is deposed or he is dead, apes and hogs will be imposed on you as rulers (Maqāṣid-i-Ḥasana)

"Your deeds are your rulers," is a well known proverb. Some people accept the proverb even as a Tradition. Meaning thereby is: As your deeds are, so shall the rulers be imposed on you. The Holy Prophet Ṣallallāhu 'Alaihi Wa Sallam! says, "Any one who fears Allah the Almighty, He creates his fear in everything. And any one who does not fear Allah, his heart is filled with the fear of every thing." (Durr-i-Manṭhūr)

I don't wish to incorporate all such statements here. I would only like to explain through examples that all sorts of troubles and sufferings that have befallen us and the Muslims are involved in them, the Holy Prophet's (Ṣallallāhu 'Alaihi Wa Sallam!) statements contain warnings on all of them and the books of Traditions are full of such topics. The Holy Prophet Ṣallallāhu 'Alaihi Wa Sallam! has clearly said that Allah Ta'ālā's disobedience causes hardships in both the worlds and the good deeds result even in the goodness of this world. Then, it has also been detailed which particular sins result in what particular troubles and sufferings and which particular obedience and submission result in which particular rewards. We excessively complain about hardships and always expect rewards but the deeds which cause them we remain quite neglectful thereof. Further, we oppose good deeds and give them up intentionally and any one who objects to this practice of ours is extremely disgraced. Our example is exactly like that of a person who suffers from diarrhoea and after every two hours takes 25 grams of scammony and still complains that he is not cured of the illness. If some one forbids him from taking scammony, he calls him a fool. How astonishing it is that if an ordinary physician declares any thing harmful, no one takes it. When a doctor who does not believe in Allah Ta'ālā declares that guava-eating spreads cholera these days, even the brave among us would not dare eat guava. A sweeper announces that there is a big black snake in a lane, the bravest man would dare not go there. An illiterate villager tells that a lion is sitting on a particular road, no one would go there. To go there in the company of some persons and armed with guns is treated an act of great bravery. But what a great tragedy it is that Allah's righteous and Holy Prophet Ṣallallāhu 'Alaihi Wa Sallam!, our most affectionate physician and most kind guardian, who is always anxious for the betterment of his Ummat and looks for it, enjoins upon the Ummat what are gainful deeds and forbids from what are harmful deeds, yet the Ummat with all its tall proclamations of devotion and dedication cares little about his advice. If the law lays down ten years' jail for a particular type of speech or writing, the brave and successful leaders and editors will deliver speeches and write articles with utmost care and attention. But the Lord of the Universe and the King of kings in Whose control are all the governments and kings sternly commands and declares in the Holy Qur'ān war from His side with one who charges interest and, in the Traditions, announces His war on those who oppose and are hostile to Allah-loving and pious people, He curses those who enter into transactions involving interest and persons trading in wine, yet how many persons are moved even a little by that. We never bother what we do and what troubles and sufferings are to follow as a result of such deeds. Let each person think for himself and it needs no telling any one else. Not only that we do not give up such deeds, there is a constant increase in them ; then we must be ready to fight against Allah and to accept curse from Him and His Prophet Ṣallallāhu 'Alaihi Wa Sallam!, and to bear sufferings and troubles, and to suffer calamities and humiliation.

WARNING

Here a suspicion arises in the mind of the common man

and even of some of the elite that good and bad deeds that have been referred to above are advantageous and harmful as much for Muslims as for the Unbelievers (and it should be so, as a harmful thing naturally causes harm), then why the Unbelievers, being involved in all bad deeds, are prosperous, accredited and well-advanced, and the Muslims are miserable and wretched and their anxieties and sufferings are on the increase ? Some fools are so much caught in the suspicion that having gone astray they refuse even to accept all the Traditions and the Divine Laws and seeing the Unbelievers enjoy the worldly gains, they accepted worldly things as a real means of betterment and gains. But in reality, the suspicion arises because of the ignorance of Islamic teachings. There is nothing that has not been elaborately dealt with in Islamic teachings and the righteous statements of the Holy Prophet Ṣallallāhu 'Alaihi Wa Sallam!. But unfortunately none has time to study them. The Holy Prophet Ṣallallāhu 'Alaihi Wa Sallam! says : One Messenger (Alaihi-Assalām) raised this very doubtful point before Allah Ta'ālā saying, "O Allah ! One of Your servants is a Muslim. He does some good deeds also. But You take away worldly gains from him and impose trials on him. There is another person who does not believe in You and also disobeys You but You take away calamities from him and give him worldly gains." Allah the Almighty revealed to him, "My Mūmin servant commits some misdeeds for which I treat him like this so that (no punishment is left for the Hereafter and) when he comes to Me, I may reward him for his good deeds only. And the Unbeliever too does some good deeds for which I treat him like this so that (no reward is left for the Hereafter and) when he comes to Me, I may punish him for bad deeds only." (Majma'

Alzawāid) A Tradition runs: Allah the Almighty never neglects any Mūmin's goodness. The Mūmin is recompensed (for his good deeds with gains and successes) in this world also and is rewarded in the Hereafter too. The Unbeliever, for his good habits, is paid back by sustenance in this very world and when he reaches the Hereafter (in the absence of Imān which is a precondition for the future reward of actions), having no virtues he is not rewarded at all.

Another Tradition says: When Allah the Almighty desires goodness for some one, He pays back for his sins in the world (as the Wrath in the world is by all means lesser than that of the Hereafter) and when He desires to punish some one severely, the punishment for his sins is stopped in this world and he is recompensed in the Hereafter.

The topic has been discussed and elucidated in the Traditions in various ways that as there is no reward for the Unbeliever in the Hereafter, he is rewarded for all sorts of good deeds in this very world. Hence, for any number of good deeds, the Unbeliever gets successes and gains in the world and the Muslim, for whom the real reward is in the Hereafter and whose evil deeds are mostly recompensed in the world, suffers usually with afflictions in this life; the more he is indulged in sins and crimes the more he has to pay for it. The Holy Prophet Ṣallallāhu 'Alaihi Wa Sallam! says: (This Ummat of mine enjoys by virtue of and through the Holy Prophet Ṣallallāhu 'Alaihi Wa Sallam! the special favours of Allah the Almighty.) There is no (everlasting) Chastisement for it in the Hereafter. Chastisement to it comes in this life (Mūmin is usually punished for his sins in this world) in the form of afflictions, trials, earthquakes and killings. Here, one doubt perplexes the historians. They find that certain communities as long as they remained indulged in encouraging atheism, no heavenly wrath was imposed on them but as and when their religious condition somewhat improved, the heavenly wrath was imposed on them. This statement is self-explanatory. There is an explicit answer to their doubt in this very statement. For, it is most probable that their deteriorating conditions might have landed them on the verge of Kufr (Unbelieving) and have caused the deferment of Divine Wrath for the Hereafter. And when they, later on, recovered from their negligence and improved their condition, they deserved to be purified through immediate punishment. Any eruption beyond operation stage is never operated upon. A surgical operation is done only when it is hoped to be helpful.

Bukhārī, Muslim and such other sources of Traditions, while narrating the story of anger of the Holy Prophet Ṣallallāhu 'Alaihi Wa Sallam! with his wives, quote Ḥaḍrat 'Umar (Raḍiyallāhu 'Anhu!) to have said, "I paid a visit to his (Ṣallallāhu 'Alaihi Wa Sallam!) house. I saw that the total assets of the house were confined to three or four things—a few handfuls of barley in one corner, one or two pieces of untanned leather and a few other triffle things in another corner. The Holy Prophet Ṣallallāhu 'Alaihi Wa Sallam! was lying on a mat, even the cloth-sheet (which he would usually wear) was not on his body nor was any cloth spread on the mat with the result that impressions of fibres of the mat were visible on his body. Seeing such a sight, I wept out. The Holy Prophet Ṣallallāhu 'Alaihi Wa Sallam! enquired why I was weeping. I humbly replied : "O Allah's Messenger! Why shouldn't I weep? The impressions of the mat are visible on your body and the whole asset of your house is before me. The people of Persia and Rome, on the other hand, do not worship Allah Ta'āla, yet they enjoy a lot of luxuries and your condition is what I am looking at with my own eyes. The Holy Prophet Ṣallallāhu 'Alaihi Wa Sallam! who was lying leaning against a pillow sat down and said firmly, "O 'Umar, the son of Khattāb ! Are you still in doubt that their good deeds have been rewarded in this world." The Holy Qur'ān says :

وَلَوْلَآ اَنْ يَّكُوْنَ النَّاسُ اُمَّةً وَّاحِدَةً لَّجَعَلْنَا لِمَنْ يَّكْفُرُ بِالرَّحْمٰنِ لِبُيُوْتِهِمْ
سُقُفًا مِّنْ فِضَّةٍ وَّمَعَارِجَ عَلَيْهَا يَظْهَرُوْنَ وَلِبُيُوْتِهِمْ اَبْوَابًا وَّسُرُرًا
عَلَيْهَا يَتَّكِـُٔوْنَ وَزُخْرُفًا وَاِنْ كُلُّ ذٰلِكَ لَمَّا مَتَاعُ الْحَيٰوةِ الدُّنْيَا وَالْاٰخِرَةُ
عِنْدَ رَبِّكَ لِلْمُتَّقِيْنَ ۝ —— (زخرف، ع ٣)

"And were it not that (all) men might become of one (evil) way of life, We would provide for every one that blasphems against (God) Most Gracious, silver roofs for their houses, and (silver) stairways on which to go up, and (silver) door to their houses, and thrones (of silver) on which they recline, and also adornments of gold. But all this were nothing but conveniences of the present life; the Hereafter in the sight of thy Lord, is for the righteous."

(Sūrah Zukhruf. Sec. 3)

The prayer of the Holy Prophet Ṣallallāhu 'Alaihi Wa Sallam! is : O Allah! Any person who believes in You and testifies me as Your Prophet, bless him with love of seeing You; make the fate easier on him and provide him with lesser worldly things and one who does not believe in You and does not accept me as Your Prophet, do not create in him love of seeing You and provide him with much more worldly things.

(Majma'ul-Zawā'id, 286/10)

It is reported in a Tradition that Allah the Almighty has said : Were it not so that Mūmins would be distressed (seeing too many comforts of others in comparision to their own troubles), I would have covered the Unbelievers (Kāfirs) with iron sheeth that they would never bear any trouble and I would have flown the world on them. (Durr-i-Manthūr) And all this for the simple reason that the world is the meanest of all.

The Holy Prophet Ṣallallāhu 'Alaihi Wa Sallam! said: If the world would be to Allah Ta'ala even worth a feather of the mosquito, the Unbeliever would not have got even a drop of water. (Dur)

Once the Holy Prophet Ṣallallāhu 'Alaihi Wa Sallam! was going somewhere. A corpse of a kid without ears was lying on the way. The Holy Prophet Ṣallallāhu 'Alaihi Wa Sallam! said, "Who is ready to buy it for a Dirham (about 25 paise)?" The companions (Raḍiyallāhu 'Anhum!) humbly spoke, "No one would like to have it even free of cost (as it would give no profit)." The Holy Prophet Ṣallallāhu 'Alaihi Wa Sallam! said, "The world is to Allah Ta'ālā much less worthless than even this." (Mishkāt quotes from Muslim)

These Traditions (Aḥādith) lead to the conclusion that since there is no value of the world to Allah and since the end of the Unbelievers is solely the world, Allah the Almighty recompenses them in the world itself for their good deeds according to their wishes. A Muslim on adopting Islam as his religion gets his title to the permanent betterment of the Hereafter; he may be involved in numberless sins but he is destined sooner or later to enjoy the blessings of the Heaven; it may be after going through the punishment for his sins or being fortunately forgiven for his sins. Hence, for his bad deeds he is usually put to afflictions and sufferings in this world. If he is not then there is an apprehension of danger for him.

The Holy Prophet Ṣallallāhu 'Alaihi Wa Sallam! says: When

you see some one involved in bad deeds and sins yet enjoying bounties of the world, then it is Istidrāj (i.e. deferment of punishment and respite from Allah). Then the Holy Prophet Sallallāhu 'Alaihi Wa Sallam! recited the following Verse from the Holy Qur'ān :

فَلَمَّا نَسُوا مَا ذُكِّرُوا بِهٖ فَتَحْنَا عَلَيْهِمْ اَبْوَابَ كُلِّ شَيْءٍ حَتّٰۤى اِذَا فَرِحُوْا
بِمَاۤ اُوْتُوْۤا اَخَذْنٰهُمْ بَغْتَةً فَاِذَا هُمْ مُّبْلِسُوْنَ ۝ —— (الانعام ع ٥)

"But when they forgot the warning they received, We opened to them the gates of all (good) things, until in the midst of their enjoyment of our gifts on a sudden We called them to account, when lo! they were plunged in despair!" (Sūrah An'ām, Sec. 5)

The Holy Prophet Ṣallallāhu 'Alaihi Wa Sallam! says, "A Mūmin is like a field which air swings hither and thither. The Mūmin is likewise shaken with troubles and sufferings. And the Unbeliever is similar to a pinetree which does not move by air and keeps on standing erect till all of a sudden it falls down uprooted." (Mishkāt)

And there are still many other texts which clearly elucidate that enjoyment of the Unbelievers is either for letting them go on committing sins or on account of some of their good deeds. Hence, any member or community of Unbelievers that does good deeds is most likely to progress and prosper and it will not be taken to task here for its ordinary sins while the Muslims are accounted here even for their ordinary sins. Therefore, the more Muslims collectively or individually commit sins, the more troubles and anxieties, reverses and humiliation they might have to suffer. The only remedy to avoid afflictions is to desist from sins and try to save others also from sins.

A Tradition says, "Trials are attached with a Mūmin—he is tried in his person, his property and children etc—till he is atoned for all his bad deeds and he passes away from this world completely free from the burden of sins." (Mishkāt quoting Tirmidhī)

In anotner Tradition it is stated, "When Allāh Ta'ālā desires "Khair" (good & welfare) for some one, He requits him of his crimes in this world and when with some one (on account of his excessive bad deeds) He desires "Sḥar" (bad), He stops afflictions from him (and lets him go on with his sins) in this world in order to recompense him fully in the Hereafter." (Mirskāt quoting Tirmiḍhī).

The oppression, tyranny, extreme dissolution and debauchery are however such crimes for which even the Unbelievers are called to account in this world. Similarly, when they exceed in moking and ridiculating the Messengers of Allah Ta'ālā, they are caught by Allah. In this state of affairs Allah the Almighty never gives respite and the encompassing penalty befalls them. The events narrating destruction of communities that have been quoted in the Holy Qur'ān are the clear proof and witness to it. Likewise the events relating to the fall of empires and kingdoms that history tells us doubtlessly prove this rule i.e. that as and when a community falls through excessive tyrannies, heavenly scourge to assist the oppressed was aroused. So says Allah the Almighty : I listen to the call of the oppressed and accept his call readily, let him be an Unbeliever. Therefore, it must be realised that ministers, administrators, officers and the rich etc. whosoever oppresses (does injustice to) his subordinates, in reality, oppresses none but himself and creates with his own hands the causes that lead him to ruin and total annihilations. Oppressions, individual or collective, are surely bound to bring dreadful results. And such oppressors once caught into quagmire (marsh) of Divine revenge, they are not likely to cross it easily.

It does not need any detailed discussions nor the space permits. The causes of the fall and destruction of empires and big nations are all elucidations of it and the history is full of it. Here I have to emphasise only that the causes of successes for the Muslims and the Unbelievers are not the same, Allah the Creatar has Himself separated them. It is only ignoranee and unawareness of the religion and the Holy Qur'ān and also of the Traditions that causes us to think in each and every case that whatever brings success for Unbelievers, prosperity for Muslims also, and any thing that does not hinder Unbelievers' success is also harmless for the Muslims. Take it to your heart that the real place for the punishment of Unbelievers' sins is the Hereafter and it is met out to them sometimes due to certain reasons in this world also; and for their good deeds and merits Allah the Almightly, the Just King definitely rewards them but in this world only and not in the Hereafter. This point is quite reasonable, for when they (Unbelievers) themselves reject the Hereafter then why the bounties of the Hereafter should be bestowed upon them. They should not be given any good fruits there but their lot in the Hereafter should be only the punishment for the rejection of the Hereafter. Therefore, Allah the Almighty says :

"Taste ye the penalty of the Fire, the which ye were wont to reject as false."

This point has been stated a number of times in the Holy Qur'ān which at a place says:

"And on the Day that the Unbelievers will be placed before

the Fire, (It will be said to them) : Ye received your good things in the life of the world, and ye took your pleasure out of them; but today shall ye be recompensed with a Penalty of humiliation, for that ye were arrogant on earth without just cause, and that ye (ever) transgressed."

(Sūrah Aḥqāf, Sec. 2)

Briefly, I draw your attention to a few sections of the Holy Qur'ān. For their commentaries, cusult authentic sources.

(١) أُولٰٓئِكَ الَّذِيْنَ اشْتَرَوُا الْحَيٰوةَ الدُّنْيَا بِالْاٰخِرَةِ ــــ (بقرة، ع ١٠)

1. "These are the people who buy the life (gains) of this world at the price of the Hereafter."

(Sūrah Baqarah, Sec. 10)

(٢) فَمِنَ النَّاسِ مَنْ يَّقُوْلُ رَبَّنَآ اٰتِنَا فِي الدُّنْيَا وَمَا لَهٗ فِي الْاٰخِرَةِ
مِنْ خَلَاقٍ ۝ ــــ (بقرة، ع ٢٥)

2. There are men who say: "Our Lord! give us (They Bounties) in this world!" But they will have no portion in the Hereafter. (Sūrah Baqarah, Sec. 25)

(٣) زُيِّنَ لِلَّذِيْنَ كَفَرُوا الْحَيٰوةُ الدُّنْيَا وَيَسْخَرُوْنَ مِنَ الَّذِيْنَ اٰمَنُوْا
وَالَّذِيْنَ اتَّقَوْا فَوْقَهُمْ يَوْمَ الْقِيٰمَةِ وَاللّٰهُ يَرْزُقُ مَنْ يَّشَآءُ
بِغَيْرِ حِسَابٍ ۝ ــــ (بقرة، ع ٢٦)

3. "The life of this world is alluring to those who reject Faith, and they scoff at those who believe. But the righteous will be above them on the Day of Resurrection: God bestows His abundance without measure on whom He will." (Sūrah Baqarah, Sec. 26)

It is said in a Hadīth that God the Great provides that

person with the world He loves and provides even that person too whom He does not love. But the Dīn (Religion) is given only to that person whom He loves. So, any person who is given Dīn is dear to Allah the Almighty. (Ḥākim)

(۴) قُلْ مَتَاعُ الدُّنْيَا قَلِيلٌ وَالْآخِرَةُ خَيْرٌ لِّمَنِ اتَّقٰى وَلَا
تُظْلَمُونَ فَتِيلًا ○ — (نسآء، ۱۱)

4. Say, "Short is the enjoyment of this world; The Hereafter is the best for those who do right: Never will ye be dealt with unjustly in the very least."

(Sūrah Nisā' Sec. 11)

(۵) وَمَا الْحَيٰوةُ الدُّنْيَا إِلَّا لَعِبٌ وَّلَهْوٌ وَلَلدَّارُ الْآخِرَةُ خَيْرٌ لِّلَّذِينَ
يَتَّقُونَ أَفَلَا تَعْقِلُونَ ○ — (انعام، ع ۴)

5. "What is the life of this world but play and amusement? But best is the Home in the Hereafter, for those who are righteous. Will ye not then understand?"

(Sūrah An'ām, Sec. 4)

(۶) وَذَرِ الَّذِينَ اتَّخَذُوا دِينَهُمْ لَعِبًا وَّلَهْوًا وَّغَرَّتْهُمُ الْحَيٰوةُ
الدُّنْيَا — (انعام، ۸)

6. "Leave alone those who take their religion to be mere play and amusement, and are deceived by the life of this world."

(Sūrah An'ām, Sec. 8)

(۷) تُرِيدُونَ عَرَضَ الدُّنْيَا وَاللّٰهُ يُرِيدُ الْآخِرَةَ - (انفال، ع ۹)

7. "Ye look for the temporal goods of this world: but Allah looketh to the Hereafter."

(Sūrah Anfāl, Sec. 9)

(٨) أَرَضِيتُم بِالْحَيٰوةِ الدُّنْيَا مِنَ الْاٰخِرَةِ فَمَا مَتَاعُ الْحَيٰوةِ
الدُّنْيَا فِي الْاٰخِرَةِ اِلَّا قَلِيْلٌ ○ —— (توبة، ع ٦)

8. "Do ye prefer the life of this world to the Hereafter? But little is the comfort of this life, as compared with the Hereafter." (Sūrah Taubah, Sec. 6)

(٩) مَنْ كَانَ يُرِيْدُ الْحَيٰوةَ الدُّنْيَا وَزِيْنَتَهَا نُوَفِّ اِلَيْهِمْ اَعْمَالَهُمْ
فِيْهَا وَهُمْ فِيْهَا لَا يُبْخَسُوْنَ ○ اُولٰٓئِكَ الَّذِيْنَ لَيْسَ لَهُمْ فِي الْاٰخِرَةِ
اِلَّا النَّارُ وَحَبِطَ مَا صَنَعُوْا فِيْهَا وَبٰطِلٌ مَّا كَانُوْا يَعْمَلُوْنَ ○ (هود، ع ٢)

9. "Those who desire the life of the Present and its glitter,—to them We shall pay (the price of) their deeds therein,—without diminution. They are those for whom there is nothing in the Hereafter but the Fire: Vain are the designs they frame therein, and of no effect are the deeds that they do!" (Sūrah Hūd, Sec.2)

(١٠) اَللّٰهُ يَبْسُطُ الرِّزْقَ لِمَنْ يَّشَآءُ وَيَقْدِرُ وَفَرِحُوْا بِالْحَيٰوةِ الدُّنْيَا
وَمَا الْحَيٰوةُ الدُّنْيَا فِي الْاٰخِرَةِ اِلَّا مَتَاعٌ (رعد، ع ٣)

10. "God doth enlarge, or grant by (strict) measure, the Sustenance (which He giveth to whomsoever He pleaseth. (The worldly) rejoice in the life of this world; But the life of this world is but little comfort in the Hereafter." (Sūrah Ra'd, Sec. 3)

(۱۱) مَنْ كَانَ يُرِيْدُ الْعَاجِلَةَ عَجَّلْنَا لَهٗ فِيْهَا مَا نَشَآءُ لِمَنْ
نُّرِيْدُ ثُمَّ جَعَلْنَا لَهٗ جَهَنَّمَ يَصْلٰهَا مَذْمُوْمًا مَّدْحُوْرًا ○ وَمَنْ اَرَادَ
الْاٰخِرَةَ وَسَعٰى لَهَا سَعْيَهَا وَهُوَ مُؤْمِنٌ فَاُولٰٓئِكَ كَانَ سَعْيُهُمْ
مَّشْكُوْرًا ○ كُلًّا نُّمِدُّ هٰٓؤُلَآءِ وَهٰٓؤُلَآءِ مِنْ عَطَآءِ رَبِّكَ ؕ وَمَا كَانَ
عَطَآءُ رَبِّكَ مَحْظُوْرًا ○ (بنی اسرائیل، ع ۲)

11. "If any do wish for the transitory things (of this life), We readily grant them—such things as We will, to such persons as We will; in the end have We provided Hell for them; they will burn therein, disgraced and rejected. Those who do wish for the (things of) the Hereafter, and strive therefor with all due striving, and have Faith,—they are the ones whose striving is acceptable (to Allah). Of the bounties of thy Lord We bestow freely on all—these as well as those; the bounties of thy Lord are not closed (to any one)".

(Sūrah Banī Isrā'īl, Sec. 2)

(۱۲) وَلَا تَمُدَّنَّ عَيْنَيْكَ اِلٰى مَا مَتَّعْنَا بِهٖۤ اَزْوَاجًا مِّنْهُمْ زَهْرَةَ الْحَيٰوةِ
الدُّنْيَا لِنَفْتِنَهُمْ فِيْهِ ؕ وَرِزْقُ رَبِّكَ خَيْرٌ وَّاَبْقٰى ○ (طٰہٰ، ع ۸)

12. "Not strain thine eyes in longing for the things We have given for enjoyment to parties of them, the splendour of the life of this world, through which We test them; But the provision of thy Lord is better and more enduring."

(Sūrah Ṭā-Hā, Sec. 8)

(۱۳) اَفَمَنْ وَّعَدْنٰهُ وَعْدًا حَسَنًا فَهُوَ لَاقِيْهِ كَمَنْ مَّتَّعْنٰهُ مَتَاعَ
الْحَيٰوةِ الدُّنْيَا ثُمَّ هُوَ يَوْمَ الْقِيٰمَةِ مِنَ الْمُحْضَرِيْنَ ○ (قصص، ع ۷)

13. "Are (these two) alike?—One to whom We have made a goodly promise, and who is going to reach its (fulfilment), and one to whom We have given the good things of this life, but who, on the Day of Judgment to be among those brought up (for punishment)?"

(Sūrah Qaṣaṣ, Sec. 7)

(۱۴) قال الذين يريدون الحيوة الدنيا يليت لنا مثل ما اوتي قارون انه لذو حظ عظيم ۝ وقال الذين اوتوا العلم ويلكم ثواب الله خير لمن امن وعمل صالحا ولا يلقها الا الصابرون ۝ (قصص، ع ۸)

14. "Said those whose aim is the life of this world: "Oh ! that we had the like of what Qārūn has got ! For he is truly a lord of mighty good fortune !" But those who had been granted (true) knowledge said: "Alas ! for you! The reward of God (in the Hereafter) is best for those who believe and work righteousness: but this none shall attain, save those who steadfastly persevere (in good)."

(Sūrah Qaṣaṣ, Sec. 8)

(۱۵) تلك الدار الاخرة نجعلها للذين لا يريدون علوا في الارض ولا فسادا والعاقبة للمتقين ۝ (قصص، ع ۹)

15. "That Home of the Hereafter We shall give to those who intend not high-handedness or mischief on earth; and the End is (best) for the righteous." (Sūrah Qaṣaṣ, Sec. 9)

(۱۶) ان وعد الله حق فلا تغرنكم الحيوة الدنيا ولا يغرنكم بالله الغرور ۝ —— (لقمان، ع ۴ - فاطر، ع ۱)

16. "Verily, the promise of Allah is true; Let not then this present life deceive you, nor let the Chief Deceiver deceive you from God the Almighty."

(Sūrah Luqman, Sec. 4)

(١٧) مَنْ كَانَ يُرِيْدُ حَرْثَ الْاٰخِرَةِ نَزِدْ لَهٗ فِىْ حَرْثِهٖ ۚ وَمَنْ كَانَ
يُرِيْدُ حَرْثَ الدُّنْيَا نُؤْتِهٖ مِنْهَا وَمَا لَهٗ فِى الْاٰخِرَةِ مِنْ نَّصِيْبٍ ۝ (شوریٰ ع ٣)

17. "To any that desires the tilth of the Hereafter, We give increase in his tilth, and to any that desires the tilth of this world, We grant somewhat thereof, but he has no share or lot in the Hereafter" (Sūrah Shūrā, Sec. 3)

All the above and many more Sections of the Holy Qur'ān refer to this very topic that the ultimate aim of the Unbelievers is the worldly life alone. The benefits of this world are real benefits in their eyes. They do not believe in the Hereafter. And, if some sects among them have faith, they do not come up to the standard of fulfilling the condition of believing in the Hereafter. The Faith is incomplete; therefore, whatever they get from God the Great, they get in this very world. Whatever good deeds they do, the fruit thereof is given in this world. Some one asked the Scholar of the Ummat (Ḥibrul-Ummat), Ḥaḍrat Ibn-i-'Abbās (Raḍiyallāhu 'Anhu!) the meaning of Sūrah Hūd's Section"

مَنْ كَانَ يُرِيْدُ الْحَيٰوةَ الدُّنْيَا

He stated that the price of their good deeds is paid in bodily good health and enjoyment through children and wealth.

Remember that it does not mean that Allah the Almighty is bound to compensate them in this world. This Section of

Sūrah Hūd is also governed by the condition explained in the Section of Sūrah Banī Isrā'il i.e.

مَنْ كَانَ يُرِيدُ الْعَاجِلَةَ

where the recompense is stated to depend solely on the will of Allah ; none has power to force Him. Ḥaḍrat Sa'īd Bin Jubair (Radiyallāhu 'Anhu!) is reported to have given the same explanation of this Section of the Sūrah Hūd that their good deeds are rewarded in this world. Ḥaḍrat Qatādah (Radiyallāhu 'Anhu!) is also stated to have offered the very explanation of this Section that Allah the Almighty pays (the price of) their good deeds in this world and by the time they reach the Hereafter, there is no good deed that remains unrewarded. And for Mūmins (Believers) their good deeds are rewarded in this world as well as (by virtue of their Imān) in the Hereafter. The same explanation is reported from Ḥaḍrat Mujāhid that the Unbelievers for their good deeds are fully recompensed in this world. Ḥaḍrat Maimūn Bin Mehran (Raḍiyallāhu 'Anhu!) said that anyone who wished to know his status in the eyes of Allah must look into his own deeds for he would reach his own deeds (i.e. he is treated in accordance with his deeds). Let him be a Mūmin or an Unbeliever, whatever good deeds he does he is certainly recompensed for them. The Mūmin is rewarded in this world and the Hereafter both, whereas the Unbeliever is paid back merely in this world. (Durr-i-Manthūr)

In his commentary of Sūrah Zilzāl's Section

فَمَنْ يَعْمَلْ مِثْقَالَ ذَرَّةٍ خَيْرًا يَرَهُ ۝ وَمَنْ يَعْمَلْ مِثْقَالَ ذَرَّةٍ شَرًّا يَرَهُ ۝

(Then shall anyone who has done an atom's weight of good,

see it. And any one who has done an atom's weight of evil, shall see it;) Ḥaḍrat Muḥammad Bin Ka'b stated that an Unbeliever who has done an atom's weight of good is certainly recompensed in this world through his own body, progeny and family i e. through physical health and financial prosperity, so much so that when he leaves this world their is no good deed that remains unrewarded. And for a Mūmin who has done an atom's weight of evil is mostly punished for the same in this world through his own body, progeny and family i.e. through various physical and financial afflictions, so much so that he may leave this world in such a state that no evil of his remains unpunished. (Durr-i-Manthūr)

It is why the Holy Prophet Ṣallallāhu 'Alaihi Wa Sallam ! says

"This Ummat of mine enjoys a special mercy of Allah Ta'ālā. It does not have (much of) Wrath in the Hereafter. Penalty for its evils is (in the form of) trials, afflictions, earthquakes, killings and other hardships in this world."

Another Tradition states, "Penalty in the Hereafter from this Ummat of mine which enjoys a special Mercy of Allah Ta'ālā has been removed. It is put, in this world, to self punishment which comes from one another."

It is said in a Tradition, "The penalty for my Ummat is in this world". In another Tradition it is stated, "Allah the Almighty has reserved chastisement of this Ummat in this world." (Majma'uz-Zawāid)

All these Traditions tell us that much of the recompense of this Ummat's sins is given in this world and this is His Mercy. Were it not so that despite multitude sins on our part we would not have been put to troubles and afflictions, it would have been more dangerous. Hence, it is clear that for the

Ummat, the followers of Ḥaḍrat Muḥammad Ṣallallāhu 'Alaihi Wa Sallam ! the only remedy for escaping the ignomy and for removing all sorts of calamities and distress lies solely in desisting with utmost care and attention from sins and bad deeds and to weep for sins committed per chance (unintentionally) and implore the Forgiveness of Allah Ta'ālā for them. There is no way out at all except this one. This can never happen that Muslims being Muslims continue to prosper and progress with multitude sins. On the contrary, the Unbelievers inspite of their hundreds of sins are granted prosperity and progress in this world as a recompense for their good deeds, however insignificant it may be.

Ḥaḍrat Sulaimān Bin 'Āmir asked the Holy Prophet Ṣallallāhu 'Alaihi Wa Sallam!, "My father was regardful of cogational relationship, particular in keeping his promise and would entertain the guests with much formality and hospitality. Will these deeds be of any use to him ?" The Holy Prophet Ṣallallāhu 'Alaihi Wa Sallam! enquired, "Did he die before the advent of Islam ?" When he replied in the positive, the Holy Prophet Ṣallallāhu 'Alaihi Wa Sallam! stated, "He (your father) would not be benefited (in the Hereafter). However, his descendants will be benefited. You people will not suffer humiliation, disgrace or poverty by virtue of your deceased father's good deeds." (Durr)

The Tradition last mentioned explanins why we find some Unbelievers progress and prosper in this world, though we may not find their deeds worthy of that. It is perhaps due to good deeds of their parents. They might be enjoying the fruits of their ancestors' good deeds.

To sum up, the bases of progress are not the same for Believers and Unbelievers alike ; some of them are common for all human beings whereas some others are peculiar to either group. The only base of the Muslims' progress is to adhere to and act upon the Islamic teachings, especially in turning back from bad deeds ; the more we are involved in sins, the more calamities are likely to encompass us in this world. Such a phenomenon that Unbelievers are enjoying prosperity despite their indulgence in similar sins should never mislead us or make us think that these sins do not hinder progress at all. It is due to this wrong supposition that we commit blunders and indulge in these sins which means nothing but inviting more and more affictions. If, in spite of our indulgence in sins, we are not put to trials, it only means respite from Allah, which Allah forbidding results in sudden and dreadful Divine Revenge.

The Holy Prophet Ṣallallāhu 'Alaihi Wa Sallam! has said, "Any person who desires to get something while remaining indulged in evil deeds he will never get that thing, and the result of his efforts will come out quite contrary to his wishes and he will get far away from what he desires and hopes to get and will come closer to what he fears (and desires to avoid). (Jāmi'ul Ṣaghīr from Ḥaḍrat Anas describing as Ṣaḥīh) Hence for Muslims while committing sins and ill-doings to expect any progress and prosperity means to remain deprived of it and to covet the Unbelievers' prosperity and to follow in their footsteps is, besides immodesty, a cause of failure. It was the tradition with the armies of Persia and Rome that the conquering army would cut off the heads of the leaders of the conquerred army and send those heads to their Chief as a sign of pride, fame and pleasure.

During the Caliphate of Ḥaḍrat Abū Bakr Ṣiddīque (Raḍiyallāhu 'Anhu!) in their battle against the Romans, the Muslims with a view to treat the enemy in a way they treated others cut off the head of a Syrian officer and sent the same to Ḥaḍrat Abū Bakr Ṣiddīque (Radiyallāhu 'Anhu!) through Ḥadrat 'Aqbah

Bin 'Āmir. When it was presented to him, Ḥaḍrat Siddīque (Radiyallāhu 'Anhu!) expressed resentment at it. Ḥaḍrat 'Aqbah said, "O the heir of the Holy Prophet Ṣallallāhu 'Alaihi Wa Sallam ! They also treat us in the same way." Ḥaḍrat Abū Bakr Ṣiddīque (Raḍiyallāhu 'Anhu!) exhorted, "Oh shall we follow the traditions and practices of the Romans and Persians ? Never bring to me any one's head. Allah's Book and the Traditions of the Holy Prophet Ṣallallāhu 'Alaihi Wa Sallam! are sufficient for us (to follow)." (Sharḥ-us-Siyar, Vol. 1)

Although the Fuqahā (Scholars of Islamic law) have declared it permissible on the basis of certain texts, yet Ḥadrat Ṣiddīque-i-Akbar's (Raḍiyallāhu 'Anhu!) opinion was not in line with them and therefore he forbade it and admonished 'Aqbah (Radiyallāhu 'Anhu!) on his considering the deeds of the Romans and the Persians as an acceptable pattern.

Once Ḥadrat 'Umar (Raḍiyallāhu 'Anhu!) was going to Syria. There was some mud and water on the way. He got down the camel, took off the leather socks and putting them on his shoulder walked through mud and water, holding the camel's cavesson in his hand. Ḥaḍrat Abū 'Ubaidah bin Jarrāh (Raḍiyallāhu 'Anhu!) said, "You have done such a thing which the Syrians very much look down upon. It is my heart's desire that the people of the city should not see you in such a condition." Ḥaḍrat 'Umar (Raḍiyallāhu 'Anhu!) clapped him on his chest and said, "Abū 'Ubaidah! Had there been some person other than you to say such a thing, I would have given him an exemplary punishment. We were obequious and Allah the Almighty bestowed honour on us through Islam. Hence, if we now seek honour through any thing other than the one through which Allah Ta'ālā honoured us, Allah the Almighty will disgrace us." (Mustadrak of Ḥākim)

Indeed the real honour for Muslims is honour from Allah

the Almighty. There is nothing to mind if this world or the people of this world take it to be disrespect or disgrace. We must seek only Allah's pleasure. A poet says :

"People take me as disrespected, disgraced or deprived of prestige but let Him not find me unsuitable for His assembly."

The Holy Prophet Ṣallallāhu 'Alaihi Wa Sallam! said, "Any person who with disobedience to Allah seeks honour among the people, the very people who praise him begin soon to despise and insult him." This point has been explained under various headings in the Maqāṣid-i-Ḥasanah. The way to success and honour for Muslim therefore is but to solicit and obtain the Pleasure of Allah the Almighty and to act upon His desires. This is the purpose of his life in this world and the real motive of his coming into this world. If there is honour (for Muslims), it is only this. If there is any gain, it is this alone. It is very surprising that although the Holy Words of Allah and true sayings of the Holy Prophet Ṣallallāhu 'Alaihi Wa Sallam ! are full of wisdom, sagacity and knowledge and explain in detail the causes of success and prosperity in both the worlds yet the Muslims look towards others for every thing. They are after offal of others. Is it not an utter disgrace and strangeness and repugnance with Allah the Almighty and His Holy Prophet Ṣallallāhu 'Alaihi Wa Sallam? Does it not resemble with that patient who in his own house has an eminent and skilful doctor but he gets himself treated by some quack or novice.

Ḥaḍrat Jābir (Raḍiyallāhu 'Anhu!) says : Once Ḥaḍrat 'Umar (Raḍiyallāhu 'Anhu!) brought a copy of the Old Testament from somewhere and said to the Holy Prophet Ṣallallāhu 'Alaihi Wa Sallam!, "O the Messenger of Allah! I have brought this Old Testament." Saying this he started reading it. The Holy Prophet Ṣallallāhu 'Alahi Wa Sallam! was displeased with it and his illuminating face was changed with frown. Seeing the serene face of the Holy Prophet Ṣallallāhu 'Alaihi Wa Sallam! changing into frown Ḥadrat Abū Bakar Ṣiddīque (Raḍiyallāhu 'Anhu!) said to Ḥadrat 'Umar (Raḍiyallāhu 'Anhu!), "Be you with death ! Don't yon see the signs of anger on the glorious face?" Ḥadrat 'Umar was busy in reading at that time. When he looked at the glorious face he was frightened and repeatedly said; "I seek refuge in Allah from His Anger and from the anger of His Prophet (Ṣallallāhu 'Alaihi Wa Sallam!), We people are contented with Allah as our Lord and with Islam as our religion and bear witness that Muḥammad Ṣallallāhu 'Alaihi Wa Sallam ! is His Apostle." The Holy Prophet Ṣallallāhu 'Alaihi Wa Sallam! exhorted, "By Him in Whose power lies my life, If Moses himself comes and you people, leaving me, follow him, you would go astray from the Right Path. If Moses 'Alaihi-Assalām were to get the period of my Prophecy, he would follow me."

The resentment of the Holy Prophet Ṣallallāhu 'Alaihi Wa Sallam! is quite understandable because so far as a full comprehensive knowledge and realisation of the Holy Book and the Traditions of the Holy Prophet Ṣallallāhu 'Alaihi Wa Sallam! is not attained, it would be dangerous for one's own religion to read any such book which is blended with right and wrong. A person who is fully aware of every pros and cons of the religion can easily and without loss of time di inguish between right and wrong. It is of no consequence for him if he reads some other book. But for a person who does not command full skill in religious knowledge (sciences of religion), there is every possibility that due to lack of knowledge he may misunderstand and believe an untrue thing to be true and consequently may go astray. As the Old Testament contained Commandments which had been abrogated by the Qur'anic laws and also there had been in it transposition or deliberate alteration of words, the Holy Prophet Ṣallallahu 'Alaihi Wa Sallam! showed great resentment on its reading lest there should happen confusion about the Islamic laws. That is why Ibni-Sīrīn (Raḍiyallāhu 'Anhu!) says, "This knowledge (knowledge of religion) is itself the religion. So look carefully what he is from whom you get your religion." (Mishkāt)

For this very reason our elders and pious preceptors always forbid adopting the company of atheists and strictly advise not to listen to speeches or read articles of such persons whose religious character is bad so that we may remain safe from the poisonous jerms of atheism. An aphorism is very often repeated: Listen carefully to what is said and never mind who said it. It is true and some Traditions also support this idea. There is a Tradition that has been narrated in different words' "A word of wisdom is like the lost property of the Mūmin. He must seize it wherever he happens to find it." (Jāmī' 'Mishkāt, Mirqāt)

But remember that it applies only to those who are well-versed in religious affairs and are able by virtue of their great insight and deep knowledge to differentiate between right and wrong. Those who have a deep and comprehensive knowledge about the bases and principles of Islam know how to scrutinise so much so that they can know and check whether what has been said is in accordance with the religion or it is contrary to it, contrary to the Holy Qur'ān and the Traditions, contrary to Islamic Jurisprudence and the exemplary lives of noble ancestors. Unless so much thorough knowledge is attained, every talk or article might impress and create dangerous effect. That is why now-a-days an impression is created in the morning and another in the evening. A person comes to the platform, impresses the audience through his oratory and makes them agree to his point of view. Then another person comes and makes an effective speech against the former's view-point and carries the audience with him.*

In short, success and prosperity for Muslims lies only in following the religion, the Tradition of the Holy Prophet Ṣallallāhu 'Alaihi Wa Sallam! and the exemplary lives of pious ancestors. This is what will be beneficial in the Hereafter. This is what causes success in this world too. The people of early period reached height of success by acting upon it and the detailed account of their lives is before us. Any person who knows history cannot deny it. To go aginst it is to go to rack and ruin and to suffer loss both in this world and the Hereafter. Let the so-called supporters of Islam prepare plans of any number they like or pass innumerable resolutions of any length ; let them publish numberless articles in the papers and be it that they are read with amazingly keen interest but all this is of no avail. The only way for progress and betterment of the Muslims is in desisting from sins and particularly in adhering to religion. There is no way other than this one that leads to destination. Here, let us think over one more point. Suppose for a moment that Islam is defaced today, all its commandments be termed as Maulviyānā Islam (Orthodoxy, Monks' religion) and Mullaic short-sightedness but is it not a fact that our ancestors, who conquerred thousands of forts, inspired thousands of millions to embrace Islam and established Islamic government in numerous regions, were the ardent believers of this very Maulviyānā Islam (Orthodoxy) and much more (so-called) short-sighted than the present Mullās. They would treat even a minor deviation from Islam a synonym to

* The Editor Maulānā Ṣadruddīn 'Amir Ansāri has very excellently elaborated this point in his book : Faḍāil-i-'Ilm Wa Manāqib-i--'Ulamā, (Virtues of Knowledge. . .) part I.

suicide. Withholding of Zakāt in their view justified the execution of death-penalty. Any one who drank wine declaring it Ḥalāl (lawful) was liable to death-penalty and one who drank it but did not refuse its unlawfulness was whipped publicly. Those people declared that only such of hyprocrates among them whose hypocracy was clearly known would dare leave Ṣalāt. It means that even all the hypocrates would not dare leave Ṣalāt. It was usual with those people that whenever some difficulty or anxiety was faced, they would immediately turn to Ṣalāt. Abū Dardā (Raḍiyallāhu 'Anhu!) says, "When the storm would blow, the Holy Prophet Ṣallallāhu 'Alaihi Wa Sallam ! would go to mosque and remain there till the storm subsided." Numerous Companions (Raḍiyallāhu 'Anhum!) have in different ways quoted this practice of the Holy Prophet Ṣallallāhu 'Alaihi Wa Sallam! that he would turn to Ṣalāt in times of difficulty and anxiety. A Companion quotes the Holy Prophet Ṣallallāhu 'Alaihi Wa Sallam! to have said that the previous Messengers' practice was also the same. The same practice is largely reported from the Companions (Raḍiyallāhu 'Anhum!) If you want to see some details, go through my booklet Faḍā'il-i-Namāz (Virtues of Ṣalāt). They enjoyed so much pleasure in prayers that while offering Ṣalāt they were shot arrows but they dared not cut short their prayers. It was their common practice to leave their shops and hurry up for Ṣalāt when they heard Adhan (Prayer call). Ḥaḍrat 'Umar (Raḍiyallāhu 'Anhu!) had sent a circular to all the governors in his empire stating, "The most revered act to me is Ṣalāt. Any one who can strictly guard it can also guard the remaining items of Islam and any one who neglects it he would much more spoil the other articles of Islam."

Ḥaḍrat Ṣiddīque-i-Akbar (Radiyallāhu 'Anhu!) sent Ḥaḍrat

Khālid (Raḍiyallāhu 'Anhu!) as the commander of the forces to wage a holy war (Jihād) against the apostates. His advice at that time was: These are the five bases—Kalimah-i-Shahādat (to bear witness that there is no God but Allah and that Ḥaḍrat Muḥammad Ṣallallāhu 'Alaihi Wa Sallam! is His Apostle), Ṣalāt (Five times prayers). Zakāt.

Ṣaum (Fasting) and Ḥajj (Pilgrimage to Mecca). Whosoever denies any one of these bases, you should fight with him. (Khamīs)

Ḥaḍrat 'Umar (Raḍiyallāhu 'Anhu!) appointed 'Atbah bin Ghazvān as the commander of the army in a battle of Persia. At that time he gave the following instructions: Be particular about piety as far as possible. Be careful about justice in pronouncing judgment. Do offer Ṣalāt at the appointed time and utter the Praises of Allah much and often.

In the days of Ḥaḍrat Abū Bakr Siddīque (Raḍiyallāhu 'Anhu!) there was a great and famous battle against the Romans at the Ajnādīn. The Romans' commander sent an Arab as spy to know the position of the Muslims and instructed him to be in their forces for one full day and night and to study carefully the position and atmosphere there. Being an Arab he could easily mix up with them. The following is the account he reported on his return:

"These people are monks at night and cavaliers during the day (i.e. they prostrate themselves in prayers before Allah the Almighty throughout the night and are on the back of horses all the day long). Even if their king's son stole some thing, his hand too would be cut off in justice and if he took to fornication, he too would be stoned to death."

The report of the spy as given above is perfectly true. It has been narrated much and often in the Books of Traditions that a woman from the Makhzūm tribe had committed theft. As she was considered to have belonged to high society, the people wished to make somehow some recommendation before the Holy Prophet Ṣallallāhu ‘Alaihi Wa Sallam! but none dared do so. Ḥaḍrat Usāma (Raḍiyallāhu ‘Anhu!)’ the son of Ḥaḍrat Zaid (Raḍiyallāhu ‘Anhu!) and adopted son of the Holy Prophet Ṣallallāhu ‘Alaihi Wa Sallam! was selected. for this work as the Holy Prophet Ṣallallāhu ‘Alaihi Wa Sallam ! loved him very much. When he recommended the case, the Holy Prophet Ṣallallāhu ’Alaihi Wa Sallam! warned him how he dared do so in the prescribed limits of Allah and then Allah’s Messenger preached a sermon in which he said, “The people of the previous Ummats were doomed to destruction for this very reason that whenever some one from gentry committed theft, he was let off. When some one from the low family did the same sin, he was punished for it. By Allah even if Muḥammad’s (Ṣallallāhu ‘Alaihi Wa Sallam!) daughter Fāṭimah (Raḍiyallāhu ‘Anhā!) were to commit theft, (May Allah save her from such blame) her hand too would have been cut off.”

Many an incident of this nature have been narrated in the Tradition Books. This was the fact that awed the hearts of the Unbelievers.

Having listened to the spy the Romans commander said, “If you have reported me their true and fair account, it is then much better to be buried under ground rather than facing them on earth.”

Once there was a Roman prisoner in the custody of the Muslims. It so happened that he got a chance and fled away. King Hercules enquired of him the position of the Muslims in so much details that their whole life may come before him. This prisoner too reported almost the same and explained that those people were monks at night and horse-riders during the day ; they would not take anything even from the Dhimmī (those Unbelievers who are their subject) without paying the price and whenever they met, they greeted each other saying Salām. Hercules retorted that if that account was true and correct, then they would become the lords of his kingdom.

During the battle of Anṭākia, Yazīd bin Abī Sufyān sent a letter to Ḥaḍrat Siddīque-i-Akbar (Raḍiyallāhu 'Anhu!)giving an account of the battle. He introduced the letter as follows: Praise be to Allah and peace be with the Holy Prophet Ṣallallāhu 'Alaihi Wa Sallam! I have the honour to state that when Hercules, the king of Rome, learnt about our advance towards him, Allah the Almighty filled his heart with fear and awe and he avoided the combat and retreated to Anṭākia. Ḥaḍrat Abū Bakr Siddīque (Raḍiyallāhu 'Anhu!) in reply wrote :

Your letter came to tell me of Hercules's overawing (and his retreat to Anṭākia). Verily Allah the Almighty has helped us like-wise by overawing the enemies and assisting us through His angels when we participated in battles under the supervision of the Holy Prophet Ṣallallāhu 'Alaihi Wa Sallam! Truly, it is the very religion to which we call the people and by virtue of which Allah the Almighty helps us by overawing the enemies. (Khamīs)

Hercules had a huge army while the number of Muslims to face him was very limited. Ḥaḍrat 'Amr bin 'Āas (Raḍiyallāhu 'Anhu!) informed Ḥaḍrat Abū Bakr Ṣiddīque (Raḍiyallāhu 'Anhu!) of the situation. In reply (Ḥaḍrat Ṣiddīque Riyḍiyallāhu 'Anhu!) wrote : You Muslims can never be defeated due to paucity of numbers. You are of course liable to be defeated inspite of your superceding the enemy in number if you are involved in sins. (Ishā'ah)

This was the real cause that had made the Muslims of that time subjugate not only the people but also sea and land, trees and mountains, birds and beasts. The books of History quote numerous instances of this phenomenon. To narrate them in details requires voluminous books. I quote a few of them.

Once a Muslim army had to camp in an African forest where all sorts of revenous and poisonous animals were in abundance. The commander of the army, Ḥaḍrat 'Aqbah with a few of Ṣaḥābah penetrated into the forest and said loudly : O the reptiles and revenous beasts of the earth ! We the Companions of the Messenger of Allah proposed to camp here. You are therefore advised to leave this place, else, if any one of you is found here afterwards, we shall kill him. This declaration worked like an electric current and made all those ferocious beasts and reptiles to leave the place in no time with all their off-springs. (Ishā'ah)

It happened once during the battles with the Romans that Ḥaḍrat Safīnah lost his way. While searching his way incidentally he came across a lion.

Ḥaḍrat Safinah (Raḍiyallāhu 'Anhu!) addressed that beast and told him that he was a servant of the Holy Prophet Ṣallallāhu 'Alaihi Wa Sallam! and that he had lost his way. The lion thereupon led him the way like a pet dog. Whenever it smelt some danger for Ḥaḍrat Safinah on the way, it would rush to remove it and come back to him again till they arrived at the camp and the lion thereafter returned to the jungle. (Mishkāt)

During the battle of Persia when the Muslims were proposing to attack Madāins, they had to cross the Tigris. The Unbelievers had removed all boats and ships from the river so that the Muslims could not use them. It was rainy season and the river was in spate. The commander of the army,

Ḥaḍrat Sa'ad ! (Raḍiyallāhu 'Anhu!) ordered his men to wade through the river. The Muslims readily obeyed. They entered the river in twos. The horses were swimming in the river towards the other bank. The adviser of Ḥaḍrat Sa'ad, Ḥaḍrat Salmān (Raḍiyallāhu 'Anhu!) would pronounce over and over again : By Allah the Almighty, verily the Almighty will help His friends and proclaim His religion over all religions and defeat the enemy so far the inequity (and adultery) does not prevail in the army and the sins do not overcome the good deeds. (Ishā'ah)

In the battle with Murtaddīn (Apostates) Ḥaḍrat Ṣiddīque-l-Akbar! (Raḍiyallāhu 'Anhu!) sent 'Alā Ḥaḍramī as the commander of an army towards Bahrain. The army passed through a jungle where water was not available at all and the soldiers were about to die of thirst. Ḥaḍrat 'Alā got off the horse, offered two Rak'ats and thereafter entreated Allah in these words :

يَاحَلِيْمُ يَاعَلِيْمُ يَاعَلِيُّ يَاعَظِيْمُ اسْقِنَا

"O the Most Forbearing ! O All-Knowing ! O the Most High ! O the Supreme in Glory ! Give us water to drink." There came instantly a cloud and rained so generously that all people drank to their fill, made their camels and horses drink and stored some in their buckets. The apostates had taken shelter (across the river) in Durban and had burnt the boats so that the Muslims could not chase them. The Muslims had to cross the river. Ḥaḍrat 'Alā reached the bank, offered two Rak'ats and prayed, "O the Most Forbearing ! O All-Knowing ! O the Most High ! O the Supreme in Glory ! Make us cross over the river." And having entreated Allah in these words, Ḥaḍrat 'Alā took the reins of his horse into his hand and jumped down into the sea. Ḥaḍrat Abū Hurairah says, "We were wading. By Allah, even the hoofs of our horses and our feet were not wet. The army consisted of four thousand soldiers." Some historians write that the level of water had lowered down so much that only the hoofs of camels and horses were drenched. There is no contradiction between the two narrations for when the army consisted of four thousand soldiers, some of them might have experienced one thing while some others like Ḥaḍrat Abū Hurairah might have crossed even without their socks being drenched. 'Afif bin Mundhir, a poet, who himself participated in this battle points in two verses to the very happening. He says : "Do you not see that Allah subjugated the river and how harsh calamity He sent down on Unbelievers ? We entreated that Exalted One Who subjugated the sea to Banī Isrā'il. He helped us much more than what He did with Banī Isrā'il.' (Khamīs)

The instances of crossing the river and sea while riding or on foot are too many. But, dear me, these are not pastime stories. They are meant to feel aggrieved of our pathetic conditions and that we must try to change it to better.

The Holy Prophet Ṣallallāhu 'Alaihi Wa Sallam! has fully explained which way leads to goodness and progress and which way leads to evils and downfall. Our pious predecessors followed him and were successful. While we neither realise the value of his words nor take any lesson from those predecessors ; we neither fear Allah nor adhere to His Holy Prophet Ṣallallāhu 'Alaihi Wa Sallam! Our expectations and aspirations with our present conduct, therefore, resemble the hopes of one who sows barley in his fields but hopes to reap wheat. The predecessors sowed wheat and so they reaped it only. Dear me, just go through the Islamic history and study every event with the eyes of your heart and take lesson therefrom. Study the instructions that were given to the armies at their departure and see how strictly they did follow them. In the bettle of Iraq which I have briefly described in Ḥikāyāt-i-Ṣaḥābah, Chapter VII (No. 6), the instructions that Ḥaḍrat 'Umar Raḍiyallāhu 'Anhu gave to the commander of the army, Ḥaḍrat Sa'ad (Raḍiyallāhu 'Anhu !) must be studied word by word. I give below the translation of a few of them. Ḥaḍrat 'Umar (Raḍiyallāhu 'Anhu!) says :

"You should not feel proud of being called maternal uncle or the Companion of the Holy Prophet Ṣallallāhu 'Alaihi Wa Sallam ! Allah the Almighty does not wipe out evil by evil but blots out evil by goodness. There is no affinity between Allah the Almighty and His slaves except the relationship of worship to Him. His rewards can be had through His obedience. It is my particular advice always to view and steadfastly follow the life of the Holy Prophet Ṣallallāhu 'Alaihi Wa Sallam! which is before you from birth to death. If you don't conform to it, your deeds will be of no avail and you will be the loser...............You are sent on a very difficult mission (the responsibilities of) which can never be completed without obedience to Him. Hence, get yourself and your colleagues accustomed to doing good deeds..................Have Allah's fear which is in two phases.................in His obedience and in abstaining from sins. And anyone who is blessed with the obedience of Allah is favoured (by creating in his heart) the indifference and hatred to the world and love for the Hereafter" (Ishā'ah). The Holy Prophet Ṣallallāhu 'Alaihi Wa Sallam! himself states, "Any person who loves this world jeopardises the Hereafter for himself. And any one loving the Hereafter, damages (apparently) this world. Hence, you must prefer that which is eternal (i.e. Hereafter) to that which is temporary (i.e. this world)."

The Holy Prophet Ṣallallāhu 'Alaihi Wa Sallam!'s Companions (Raḍiyallāhu 'Anhum!) had fully grapsed and strictly followed this principle. And it is a fact that a person who prefers the Hereafter to this world and is ready to bear the loss of this world rather than the loss of the Hereafter, he seems to suffer some worldly loss but in reality he does not, for he bears only that loss which he is destined to suffer whether he prefers this world or that. The Holy Prophet Ṣallallāhul 'Alaihi Wa Sallam! says, Any person who desires (and makes efforts for the) betterment of the Hereafter, Allah the Almighty fills his heart with contentment and makes his affairs settled in order and makes the world to him a baseless affair. And any person wishing to gain this world only, poverty overstrains his mind, his affairs get diffused and (in spite of his efforts) he does not get more than what is destined for him." (Mishkāt)

Hence, the stories of the companions Radiyallāhu 'Anhum! and the Friends of Allah explain how much they were indifferent to this world and that the meanest and the most worthless thing in their eyes was the comfort of this world. And it should be so because everything of the world has been created for them (and they were not created for the world). Once Ḥaḍrat Sa'ad sent 'Āṣim bin 'Umar as the chief of a very small contingent to conquer Maisān, a place. It so happened that when 'Āṣim bin 'Umar reached there, the provisions of the Muslims were exhausted totally and they had nothing to eat nor was any foodstuff available anywhere. They, on the edge of a jungle, came across an inhabitant of Persia who was a shepherd. When they enquired of him about the availability of milk and animals for transport, he deliberately hid the fact and told that he had no knowledge about that. But instantly an ox from within the jungle shouted : The enemy of Allah has told you a lie. We are present here (for you). On hearing it, 'Āṣim went into the jungle, brought those animals to the camp and distributed them among the soldiers.

Some historians state that the incident occurred to Ḥaḍrat Sa'ād at Qādsiah. There is no contradiction, for it is very likely that the incident might have occurred at both the occasions.

When the above stated incident was narrated to Ḥajjāj bin Yūsuf, he was so surprised and called such of the persons as were present at the the time of happening of this incident. They testified it and said that they had themselves heard the ox shouting. When enquired about people's reaction of that time about the incident they told Ḥajjāj that the people took it as a proof of Allah's pleasure with Muslims and concluded that successes were on their side. Ḥajjāj argued that it could happen only when all the soldiers of the army were fully purified and pious. They told him that they did not know what the soldiers had in mind. But as far as they had seen, they appeared to be much more pious about world than any one. No one of them was coward or dishonest nor would any one of them break his word.

The above incident claims the animals speak and present themselves for the pious and holy men. These things are not at all astonishing. As for the animals speaking to man the Ṣaḥīḥ Aḥādīth verify it. In Bukḥārī Sharīf and other books on Traditions it is stated that a person was carrying a cow. He was tired and rode on it. The cow said, "We have not been created for this work. We have been created only for fields." The people were greatly amazed at it. But the Holy Prophet Sallallāhu 'Alaihi Wa Sallam ! stated, "I, Abū Bakar and 'Umar firmly believe in it (i.e. the animal can speak to man)." Once a person was grazing goats. A wolf took away a goat. The person made a lot of hue and cry. The wolf thereupon said, "Who will look after these goats in the days of beasts (i.e. at the approach of the Dooms day) ?" Here too the Holy Prophet Sallallāhu 'Alaihi Wa Sallam! repeated the same statement : I, Abū Bakar and 'Umar firmly believe in it. (Mishkāt quoting from Bukhārī and Muslim)

The books on miracles narrate numerous incidents of this nature where it is stated that animals testified the Prophethood of the Holy Prophet Ṣallallāhu 'Alaihi Wa Sallam! and rebuked the people for not adopting Islam as their religion. If you want to read more on the subject, please go through "Shifā" by Qāḍi'Iyāḍ which contains a few of them.

Another aspect of the incident that the animals offered themselves is too quite understandable. When this group of persons was always ready to lay down their life in the way of Allah with so much willingness and great enthusiasm, then Divine Help was a natural consequence. A Persian poet says :

Do not turn away from the subservience of the Almighty so that nothing can turn away from your subservience.

Books of history are full of instances narrating how much these pious predecessors longed to sacrifice their lives for the cause of Allah. You may, if you like, see the glimpses of this unique devotion in my book "Ḥikāyāt-i-Ṣaḥābah" wherein I have mentioned a few of them as specimen.

During the Ḥajjatul Widā' (the last pilgrimage) the Holy Prophet Ṣallallāhu 'Alaihi Wa Sallam! sacrificed one hundred camels. At the time of slaughter the camels in fives and sixes would rush to him each longing to be sacrificed first by the

Messenger of Allah. This incident has been narrated in details in Abū Dā'ūd.

We find in our daily life in this world that petty and helpless officers do their best to help and defend their obedient subordinates, then why the Almighty would not help His obedient servants ? Look, He Himself promises :

يَاأَيُّهَا الَّذِينَ آمَنُوا إِنْ تَنْصُرُوا اللّٰهَ يَنْصُرْكُمْ —— (محمد، ع ۱)

"O you who believe! If you will aid (the Cause of) Allah, He will aid you, and plant your feet firmly."

(Sūrah Muḥammad, Sec. 1)

إِنْ يَنْصُرْكُمُ اللّٰهُ فَلَا غَالِبَ لَكُمْ وَإِنْ يَخْذُلْكُمْ فَمَنْ ذَا الَّذِي
يَنْصُرُكُمْ مِنْ بَعْدِهِ —— (آل عمران، ع ۱۷)

"If Allah helps you, none can overcome you; if He forsakes you, who is there, after that that can help you. In (Allah, then let Believers put their trust)."(Sūrah Āl-i-'Imrān,Sec.17)

The pious Companions (Raḍiyallāhu 'Anhum!) of the Holy Prophet Ṣallallāhu 'Alaihi Wa Sallam! had realised this fact fully. Obedience to Allah and His Holy Prophet Ṣallallāhu 'Alaihi Wa Sallam ! was their nature. Success of all kinds consequently embraced them on every occasion. Whenever there was some mistake or oversight on their part, they bore the consequences of their negligence. The battle of Uḥud and what happend therein at that time is well known. The Holy Prophet Ṣallallāhu 'Alaihi Wa Sallam! had posted a particular contingent on a certain strategic point and had directed them not to leave their post whether the battle goes in favour of the Muslims or against them. The Muslims got initial successes and almost completely overpowered the enemy. Finding the enemy fleeing, some members of the contingent thought that the Muslims had won the battle and that it was no longer necessary to stick to the post. They therefore started chasing the enemy. Their leader reminded them of the Holy Prophet Ṣallallāhu 'Alaihi Wa Sallam!'s directive but through misunderstanding they interpreted the directive to apply only in the ups and downs of the battle and not at a time when victory was in sight. As they left the post, Khālid bin Walīd who at that time was in command of the Unbelievers' forces took the opportunity and fell on the Muslims from behind through the same point. What happened thereafter is detailed in the books of history and Traditions. I need not narrate it here.

In the battle of Ḥunain the Muslims were in a larger number and a few of them felt elated of their number and uttered words of vanity. But elation is never liked by Allah and as a result the Muslims had to experience a severe trial. Allah the Almighty Himself mentions :

لَقَدْ نَصَرَكُمُ اللّٰهُ فِيْ مَوَاطِنَ كَثِيْرَةٍ وَّيَوْمَ حُنَيْنٍ اِذْ اَعْجَبَتْكُمْ كَثْرَتُكُمْ
فَلَمْ تُغْنِ عَنْكُمْ شَيْئًا وَّضَاقَتْ عَلَيْكُمُ الْاَرْضُ بِمَا رَحُبَتْ ثُمَّ
وَلَّيْتُمْ مُّدْبِرِيْنَ ۝ —— (توبہ، ع ۴)

"Assuredly Allah did help you in many battle-fields and on the day of Ḥunain, Behold! Your great numbers elated you but they availed you nought; the land for all that is wide, did constrain you, and you turned back in retreat."

(Surāh Taubah, Sec. 4)

In the battle fought to crush the forces of apostates

(Murtaddīn) the Muslims first encountered Ṭulaiḥah Kadhdhāb and crushed his force. He and many of his men fled away and some were killed. The success greatly encouraged the Muslims. Then they faced Musailmah Kadhdhāb and had a tough fight. Thousands of Musailmah's men were killed and a good number of Muslims also sacrificed their lives before they could win the battle. Ḥaḍrat Khālid (Raḍiyallāhu 'Anhu!) who was commanding the Muslim army states,

"When we had crushed Ṭulaiḥah Kadhdhāb who was not so forceful, I happened to utter a word (of vanity) and trials follow the words of vanity. I happened to say: These Banū Ḥanīfah! What they matter! They are just like those whom we have already met (and crushed). But when we faced them we found them outstanding and matchless. They fought with us untiringly from sunrise to sunset."

Ḥaḍrat Khālid, the commander himself, confesses that it was only due to one word of vanity that they had to face such a fierce encounter. That is why the pious Caliphs were very particular even about minor matters. They stressed strict observance of Sunnat in ordinary affairs as well.

When the Muslims were proceeding to attack Yarmouk, Ḥaḍrat Khālid (Raḍiyallāhu 'Anhu!) was occupied in the battle of Iraq. Ḥaḍrat Abū Bakar Ṣiddīque (Raḍiyallāhu 'Anhu!) wrote to him to appoint his successor in Iraq and to proceed immediately to help the Muslims in Yarmouk. Hadrat Ṣiddīque (Raḍiyallāhu 'Anhu!) in his letter, while appreciating Ḥaḍrat Khālid's (Raḍiyallāhu 'Anhu!) services, congratulated him on his successes and wrote,

"Be careful lest vanity should creep in you, otherwise you will stand to lose and be forsaken. Behold! You must never boast of any deed or action of yours for it is only the Almighty Who has the right of boasting and He is the Owner of reward !" (Khamīs)

We find in the speeches and writings of these pious predecessors great stress on being particular even about petty affairs and reproach on minor lapse or slip. There was strict censure and severe punishment on sins. Ḥaḍrat Khālid (Raḍiyallāhu 'Anhu!) whose brilliant character and valuable services are known to Muslims and Unbelievers both was called to account on a minor thing. Ḥaḍrat 'Umar (Raḍiyallāhu 'Anhu!) insisted on Ḥaḍrat Ṣiddīque (Raḍiyallāhu 'Anhu!) during his Khilāfat to depose Khālid (Raḍiyallāhu 'Auhu!) of his position to which Ḥaḍrat Ṣiddīque (Raḍiyallāhu 'Anhu!) did not agree. In his period Ḥaḍrat 'Umar (Raḍiyallāhu 'Anhu!) deposed Ḥaḍrat Khālid (Raḍiyallāhu 'Anhu!) of his position and ordered that he should be brought to him fettered and handcuffed only because Ḥaḍrat Khālid (Raḍiyallāhu 'Anhu!) had lavishly and abundantly rewarded a certain poet.

As Ḥaḍrat 'Umar (Raḍiyallāhu 'Anhu!) proceeded for the first time to Baitul-Muqaddas, he directed the commanders posted in the nearby areas to appoint their substitutes on their respective armies and to meet him in Jābiah. The commanders complied with the order and reached Jābiah. The first to meet Ḥaḍrat 'Umar (Raḍiyallāhu 'Anhu!) was Yazīd bin Abī Sufyān. Next came Ḥaḍrat Abū 'Ubaidah and then Ḥaḍrat Khālid. All the three commanders were wearing some sort of silken clothes. Seeing them in this dress, Ḥaḍrat 'Umar (Raḍiyallāhu 'Anhu!) dismounted and began to throw stones on them and exhorted, "How soon it is that you have deviated from your old views and dare come to see me in these clothes ! It is only for two years that you are having to your fill. If you had departed from your views after two hundred years, I would have even then replaced you by other fellows as commanders." All the three Commanders regretted the lapse and explained that as they were armed the upper cloth was simply to cover the arms. (Tabrī) (Rules for wearing silken clothes are detailed in the relevant books. Silken clothes are permitted in certain cases.)

When Maisān was conquerred, Ḥaḍrat 'Umar (Raḍiyallāhu 'Anhu!) appointed Ḥaḍrat Nu'mān bin 'Adī the governor of that place. Ḥaḍrat Nu'mān (Raḍiyallāhu 'Anhu!) wished his wife to accompany him but she did not agree to it. Reaching Maisān, Ḥaḍrāt Nu'mān wrote a loving letter to his wife wherein he sketched in verses the delightful atmosphere of Maisān and mentioned drink and its glasses in the poetical style. As Ḥaḍrat 'Umar (Raḍiyallāhu 'Anhu!) came to know of this letter, he sent a letter to Ḥaḍrat Nu'mān wherein quoting the first section of Surāh Ghāfir, he wrote :

"I came across of your so and so verse and have deposed you of your rank." Ḥaḍrat Nu'mān came to the Caliph and swore that he had never touched wine and that whatever he had written was merely figurative and poetry. Ḥaḍrat 'Umar (Raḍiyallāhu 'Anhu!) in reply said, "And so I think of you. But I shall never appoint you as governor in any area."

(Mu'jamul-Buldān)

Such were those pious predecessors in their (so-called) orthodoxy and rigidity. Books of history and Traditions quote thousands of similar instances. This character was the real cause of their success in the two worlds. Whenever there was any lapse the loss followed it, as you have just read. These instances also tell us that the warning and reproach was always according to status. The higher the person or group of persons was in position and rank the more minutely he was censured and punished for mistakes.

This was in accordance with the rule that many actions which are always treated good are (considered) bad when done by the most pious person. Sūrah 'Abas contains reproach only because a worldly rich fellow was preferred to a poor blind one, although the preference was also for the sake of religion. In contrast to the above category, the lower the group in their rank the more generously their minor oversights were forgiven. Punishment was meted to them only when their crimes exceeded the tolerable limit.

Sardāndia is a well-known island. At the time of its subjugation the cases of defalcation in looty occurred excessively. Many people without any observance of the looty-rules took whatever they could. When after victory they were sailing back there sounded a curse from an unseen source, "O Allah! Drown them all". And all were drowned.

What I said in the beginning were the words of the Holy Prophet Ṣallallāhu 'Alaihi Wa Sallam! and these events are the actual instances of those promises and threats.

Pages of history books are full of similar instances ; but (in spite of these warning words and admonishing instances) what is happening these days, is before our own eyes. We ourselves go on adopting such things as lead to atheism and dissolution; our out and out indulgence in sinful deeds is on constant increase ; and in sequel, the afflictions, trials and calamities are also on constant increase. In the circumstances, if there can be any remedy and solution for our problems it lies only in desisting from sins and in strict adherence to the religion. But, alas ! Who dares proclaim this down-trodden slogan and who cares to listen to it ? It is, hence, only Allah to Whom we can complain and it is only He Whose Help can be sought.

Wa Ākhiru Da'wānā Anil Hamdu Lillāh-i-Rabbil 'Ālimīn.